LAUGHTER IN PROVENCE

WINIFRED FORTESCUE

First published in Great Britain 1950
by Blackwood & Sons Ltd.

Published in Large Print 2001 by ISIS Publishing Ltd.
7 Centremead, Osney Mead, Oxford OX2 0ES
by arrangement with Society of Authors

British Library Cataloguing in Publication Data
Fortescue, Winifred, Lady, 1888–1951
Laughter in Provence. – Large print ed.
1. Fortescue, Winifred, Lady, 1888–1951 –
Homes and haunts – France – Provence
2. English – France – Provence
3. Large type books
4. Provence – Social life and customs – 20th century
I. Title
944.9'0815'092

ISBN 0–7531–9696–4 (hb)
ISBN 0–7531–9697–2 (pb)

Printed and bound by Antony Rowe, Chippenham and Reading

944.9
FOR

LAUGHTER IN PROVENCE

CONTENTS

1.   Provence To-Day   1

2.   The Water-Guard   21

3.   The Compleat Gardener   34

4.   The Incompleat *Bonne*   60

5.   Gamine   88

6.   Fun In Fever   101

7.   'Ullo! 'Ullo!   115

8.   We Entertain   125

9.   New Year in Provence   147

10.   "Laughter, The Divine Disinfectant"   167

CHAPTER
ONE

Provence To-Day

What extraordinary changes can take place during a lapse of ten years, particularly when a war intervenes!

When I left Provence in 1940 to share the dangers which threatened my country I had already become a familiar citizen of Opio, where my friend *Mademoiselle* of the *Château* had lived for many years, but I was the latest comer, having inhabited my little "Sunset House" only since 1935.

When I returned in 1945 I was the sole survivor of the English Colony on this little mountain. The beloved *Mademoiselle* had succumbed to malnutrition. She could not withstand the hardships and privations of Occupied France, and I know that enforced inaction when she could no longer work with and for the French Army must have broken her heart — though never her gallant spirit. Another old friend of hers, whom she had housed in a dear little stone cottage near her *Château*, had decided to live henceforth in England because she could not bear to be so near *Mademoiselle's* empty home, once the pivot of our existence, nor the rambling old house converted by *Monsieur le Marquis* (who had

1

also died in England) which flanked her little home on its other side.

Only the certainty that *Mademoiselle* wished me to come back and to continue her work for the children of Provence had given me courage to return and to strive, in loneliness, to take up the snapped golden threads of our so happy life, and try with the help of a loving and understanding God to weave them into a pattern not too unworthy of Him.

So back I came — and here I am, my life forever complicated by the absentee landlords of those empty houses — charming people, all of them — who make occasional meteoric arrivals to keep a vague eye upon their properties, and spend perhaps a fortnight here while arranging for tenants to occupy them.

I am awakened in the early morning by the shrilling of the telephone in my ear — a telegram from England. Half dazed with sleep I take up a pencil and collect my wits to transcribe it. Very few of the telephone operators in our region understand English or, if they can read it, they find great difficulty in pronouncing our language, so many of our words being spelt in one way and pronounced in another. Their attempts are gallant — and funny. We generally stop mid-way, the poor little operator stifled by giggles, and then I suggest that she spell each word.

D pour Denise, A pour Arthur, R pour Robert, L pour Louise, I pour Irene, N pour Nice, G pour Georges — ah yes! DARLING — and then follow the requests, each spelled out in the same manner, and at last I have understood my instructions and lie back upon my pillows gasping for my *petit déjeuner*.

The English are at last discovering the E.L.T. telegram — twenty-five words for the small sum of three shillings and fourpence. One sends it at night and it arrives in France with the letter-post next morning or, in my case, is telephoned at an early hour before the Post Office opens to the public.

When called upon to follow the French spelling of an English telegram on an empty tumpkin or, even worse, to telephone an urgent message of one's own to a bewildered operator I, being a wicked woman, long to spell in this way — D pour DAMN, A pour ASS, and to use all the swear-words I learned from a husband whose brothers were all in the Army or Navy, which Services (especially the latter) possess a rich and varied vocabulary of expletives.

I am informed by one or other of the absentee owners of properties that she will be arriving in our neighbourhood on a certain date, and will I be an angel and see that the water-supply and electricity are turned on, a supply of wood or coal got in, and one of our peasant friends secured as *bonne-à-tout-faire*.

I start telephoning to the Water Board and Electric Light Company and am probably told that the last tenants of that house did not pay the bills before departure (through no fault of their own, very probably, because the Water Rate is paid but once a year and the Electric Light bills once in two months, and these documents often arrive *after* the departure of tenants who, if English, then have the devil of a time with the

3

Bank of England before they can send out money to pay their debts). But until these bills are paid water ceases to flow and electric light to shine. All my blandishments are in vain and I am then obliged to telephone to our long-suffering English lawyer in Nice, who for his sins has the responsibility of solving these problems and paying unpaid bills for the absent. Perhaps being a musician helps him to make harmony where discords existed, and a knowledge of modern music which is so often made up of these discordant sounds may even make problems which he is required to solve both interesting and amusing.

We have just been through a water-crisis which occurred in a neighbour's house. It was let to five people, and as the owner had recently occupied it, everyone imagined that her full ration of water, *for which she had paid*, was flowing automatically into her reservoirs.

But knowing the ways of our Water-Guard (of whom more anon) I felt that it would be kind to verify the water-supply before these people came in, so I turned on inside and outside taps — with no result. I found the big reservoir in the garden empty, likewise the tanks in the loft.

This would be a nightmare for the incoming tenants, because I well knew that even when I had telephoned to the Water Board of our neighbouring town and they had sent a messenger to track down our Water-Guard on his wanderings and he had turned on the water, none could reach the tanks in the roof until the water in the big outside reservoir reached a certain height and the pressure was enough. To reach that level might take some days — and in the meanwhile what would five people do in a house completely devoid of water?

I had secured the services of my ex-*bonne*, Margharita, who is now married and lives in our village, to look after these friends of mine, and even her unruffled calm and dignified demeanour (so rare in an Italian servant) were completely upset by this unexpected (by her) water-crisis. How should she scrub and clean the house in preparation for the *locataires*? How cook for them? She would be unable to light the kitchen stove, for the empty hot-water tank would burst. And how could her charges wash and bathe themselves?

How indeed!

I could only suggest that she should carry down pails to the *Château* of *Mademoiselle*, also full of tenants, and draw water from its outdoor taps. Heavy work for my poor Margharita, for afterwards she must drag those pails half-way up our mountain, and this performance must be repeated several times because a bucket-full of water contains pitifully little to supply the needs of five people — plus Margharita. Added to her work as *bonne-à-tout-faire* she would be exhausted by the end of the day, but Margharita never lacked courage, and when in charge of a house and its inhabitants her pride insisted that they must be perfectly cared for.

So that when I had left her, her great eyes sombre, her thin shoulders shrugged despairingly, I knew that she would make the best of a difficult situation.

And, as reported to me daily by the wife of *Monsieur le Colonel*, the favourite niece of my John who, mercifully, possesses a glorious sense of humour and an unquenchable spirit, the situation could not have been more difficult. The *cabinets* were, of course, the nightmare; for all their tanks were dry for two awful days and nights until the water in the reservoir had risen to the necessary level.

My niece, with eyes brimming with laughter, told me that on the second morning they had heard the clanking of a chain.

Margharita, her eyes blazing with excitement, ran into the room where the four ladies were sitting, crying joyously:

"Mesdames! Monsieur le Colonel a tiré la chaine du cabinet!"

This glad news brought them all into the corridor with a rush, and the poor Colonel found five women awaiting his exit longing to hear the glad news that at last water flowed in the house — luckily he, also, possesses a sense of humour. But alas! he had pulled in vain! The tanks were still dry.

A downpour of rain proved of great assistance. Every vessel that could contain water was put out on the terrace to catch the precious drops, and everyone stood outside, faces turned heavenwards, that they might be washed by lovely soft water.

We don't realise the value of water until we lack it, as *I* found out on my first camping expedition. I had packed a lovely tea-basket with everything necessary to brew a refreshing drink of China tea — EXCEPT WATER. I was on a lonely Yorkshire moor miles from human habitation when, having lit my little spirit-lamp and filled an infuser with China tea, I discovered my idiocy. But this early experience taught me a valuable lesson.

When water really flowed from all the taps in that little house its inhabitants became almost deliriously happy. Their joy to be able to wallow once again in a luxurious, hot bath was really pathetic. I had offered them the hospitality of my bathrooms, but the weather was bad, and it is not much fun to have a warm bath and then be obliged to splash forth into a thunderstorm and be soaked again by torrential rain before reaching home, and so my repeated offers were refused. Therefore when their own hot-water system functioned their happiness knew no bounds and their past miseries became a great joke. Happy is he — or she — who can see the funny side of such crises and discomforts while they are happening. Thank God when they happen to me my midriff at once begins to shake — which I am told is the scientific explanation of laughter. This is sometimes very awkward and has often been misunderstood. Something catastrophic happens and I immediately see the funny side of it which may not be perceived by others until long after the event or, worse still, never seen at all.

During this war I was asked to take tea with a very kind old lady and her husband. While we were drinking it a relative of theirs came in with a very grave face and said:

"Lady Fortescue, I am afraid I have terribly bad news for you. I bought the evening paper in London and in it I read that the Germans have occupied the South of France. I thought at once of your home there." There was a silence as my kind host and hostess exchanged glances of shocked concern and then glanced nervously at me.

What they saw shocked them even more, for I was laughing silently as is my wont, tears of mirth coursing down my cheeks, *not* the tears of grief that they had doubtless feared to see.

"Lady Fortescue!" exclaimed my hostess. "What can you find amusing in such a tragedy?"

"Well in my case there *is* a funny side," I gasped, "and when I have explained it to you I'm sure you will laugh with me."

And then I told them that before leaving my little loved home I had let it to an Englishwoman who lived on Cap Ferrat and feared that the Coast might eventually be bombarded. With her she brought her most precious possessions leaving no room for mine. I had therefore called in some expert removal men to pack my lovely Waterford glass which had been in my family for many, many years and was given to me by my parents as their wedding present; the beautiful porcelain dinner service given to us by a relative of my husband's — pure white edged with gold and the plain Fortescue badge — the famous shield which gave the family its name — outlined in gold — my Man's most precious books — in fact, anything and everything of value in the house. These treasures were all packed as though for export in huge wooden packing-cases with mountains of protective wood-shavings and the cases then sealed and banded with steel because I intended to have them removed to the flat of a friend in Grasse which I had rented for this purpose knowing that she would guard them jealously for me. Having suffered much from my last furniture removal to my present home from our old *Domaine* — only a few miles distant (that disastrous journey chronicled in another book of mine[1]) — I had resolved that this time no such accidents should occur.

When I was told that the Germans had occupied the South of France I at once foresaw wholesale looting of every property, and in a flash I realised that I HAD PACKED FOR THE BOCHE! All *he* had to do was to label my packing-cases so beautifully packed for export — to BERLIN.

Well — if that had happened it *would* have been funny — terribly ironic, but funny all the same. However, even when I had choked forth my explanation my host and hostess continued to look both grieved — and shocked. No doubt I accentuated my reputation for eccentricity which I am sure I must have gained in that neighbourhood; for a woman who in these days openly expressed her horror of the fashionable cocktail parties, refused to attend them, and preferred to furnish and inhabit an abandoned game-keeper's cottage amid lovely woods, situated at the bottom of a precipice with no road-approach and no telephone during a war, in the fighting area of Sussex, must surely be a little mad. So perhaps my unseemly and untimely laughter may have been somewhat excused. It was certainly not understood.

Well, to return again to absentee landlords and their empty or temporarily occupied houses.

---

[1] "Sunset House" (Messrs William Blackwood & Sons Ltd.).

9

Not only are agonies caused by lack of water but also by too much water, which sometimes causes electrical complications. First I will cite my own. When *Mademoiselle* acted as my amateur architect she insisted that my electric installation should be invisible. She had a horror, as have I, of visible pipes and cables, and gave orders that my electric wires must be encased in insulated tubing and built into the solid stone walls. Any outside wiring of front door-bell, the lantern on the courtyard wall, and that placed outside the garage some distance away, must be run underground. She gave the work to a clever Russian electrician who, when the war came into our region and France collapsed, consented to go to Germany to work for the Boche and therefore could never be employed again, though he has since returned thoroughly discouraged by the treatment he received in Germany. He had done his work for my house beautifully, but no one else knew where he had placed his cables and his fuse-boxes when my first electrical troubles came upon me.

First, we found it impossible to extinguish the lantern outside the great entrance doors. I had lit it from my loggia to aid the exit of some departing friend on a dark night, and when the doors closed, switched off the light from indoors. Or so I thought ... Electricity was then severely rationed and a heavy fine imposed if one should exceed the quantity allowed. Next morning someone rang my electric bell outside the entrance to inform me that my lantern was still alight — and that he had received an electric shock when he pressed the bell.

My house is built upon the highest point of our mountain and my electric lantern had been setting a bad example to the neighbourhood all night. As the light refused to be extinguished there was nothing for it but to remove the electric bulb until an electrician could be found to come and correct the short-circuit. For Henri, my gardener, informed me there must be one, after he had inadvertently touched the wall near the gate while cutting back a too-profuse shrub, and getting a shock through his shears. *I* got one that same night when striving to heave up the heavy iron bar which secures the wooden gates from the inside. The wall was alive with electricity — most uncanny. Henri said it was because the recent rains had soaked into the porous stone. Somewhere — WHERE? — the hidden insulated cable must have worn through and a leak occurred.

Needless to say we discovered this leak on Saturday night when all electricians had gone home for the week-end, and equally, of course, the following Monday was one of the innumerable *jours de fête* when everyone was on holiday. We were roused in the small hours by a furious shrilling of the electric bell which rings in the kitchen and in the corridor upstairs outside my bedroom.

Naturally I thought that it was a summons from one of my peasant friends, and that someone was ill or dying or giving untimely birth, and that a scared relative either wanted to telephone for medical aid from my house or to beg me to drive the sufferer to the nearest hospital. They have been repeatedly urged by me to do this in case of dire need.

11

But when the bell continued to ring and ring and ring with deafening clamour I realised that we must be short-circuiting again; for my peasant neighbours are so courteous that they would never ring in so imperative a manner, keeping a finger continuously upon the bell-button.

My little Scots friend who came out to me to learn French and in return for housing, French lessons and pocket-money, to type for me, drive the car and be a general comfort to us all, came leaping upstairs wondering if *I* was dying, and wanting to dictate my last wishes hurriedly in shorthand, for I had been very ill. When I told her that it was the outdoor bell she put on a coat and ran across the courtyard to open the gates and find out for certain whether this was a real summons. To open the doors she must heave up the heavy iron bar — and *she* got an electric shock down her arm. No one stood outside, and as the bell continued to ring she pressed a bit of stick on the bell-push to see if it had stuck, but failed to make the discordant music cease. Then she slammed the great doors, but did *not* replace the iron bar, and came leaping upstairs again to report to me.

A young man recently compared her to a gazelle because of her lithe movements, her large eyes and the proud carriage of her head, and so in future I shall refer to her as the Gazelle; for since she came out to me we have shared many miseries, joys and jokes, and she will inevitably appear again when I chronicle other adventures. She now fetched a step-ladder and stifled the warning bell in the corridor with cotton-wool, then descended to the kitchen and, having exhausted her supply of cotton-wool, made some Heath Robinson device to silence the other. And for a few hours there was peace. Then the Heath Robinson contraption broke down and the kitchen bell began to ring again just under her bedroom. There followed a wild search in the store-cupboards of my linen room for more cotton-wool, which had at least partially deadened the bell in the corridor. At length a huge roll of it was discovered, the remnant of some that my husband had bought for himself when he had earache in his bachelor days. I had found this gigantic roll of cotton-wool, about the size of a large swaddled Italian *bambino*, in one of his cupboards in our suite of rooms in Windsor Castle and had asked him for what it had been bought. When he told me that it was "to bung up one of my ears when I had earache," I was at first staggered and then convulsed with laughter, for he had the smallest, neatest ears man ever had. Well, a small quantity of this roll of cotton-wool most usefully choked that noisy bell, but even then a very large quantity remains even after thirty-six years of stripping for one purpose or another.

John always bought *en gros* — part of his creed of tree "planting for posterity" perhaps. He always planned for the future, and so, I suppose, he bought enough cotton-wool to stuff the ears of himself, his wife, should he marry, and a tribe of his children, should he have any, till the end of their lives.

When he went to India with King George V. to chronicle the pageantry of the Durbar, he took with him no less than ninety-six vests. He knew that the climate would be hot and that the natives wash clothes and beat them on stones to dry them, so he allowed for one clean vest per day and decided to bring them back to England to be washed at home. When we married he told me that he did not think that *he* need buy a trousseau for himself, and when I saw that mountain of vests as a specimen of his wardrobe I cordially agreed with him.

I could not really criticise him, because I, also, am apt to buy in quantity. People coming upon me while I am striving to write a book are astonished by the mass of pencils by my side. One man inquired: "Does she collect them?" when he saw this vast quantity. I explained that I always write my manuscript in pencil so that I can rub out any mistakes and then hand a clean and corrected manuscript to my typist, and therefore I sharpen an army of pencils so that when one wears down I can pick up another and need not interrupt my train of thought to sharpen the blunt point.

Now, having visited Windsor Castle and travelled to India, we will return again to my little Sunset House and its electrical disturbances. These, as I have said, could not be put right until, at the earliest, Tuesday morning, when we might have the luck to find an electrician and, having found him, to persuade him to come to our aid. He was found — but he was sleeping off the effects of the Monday feast-day. He is an accordionist and is often engaged to play dance music in *cafés* till dawn. Then he goes home — and sleeps. When my gardener, Henri, called at the house with my urgent message, the young apprentice whispered hoarsely: "*Il dort!*" and dared not disturb him.

And so my bells continued to ring for a long week-end and my electricity bill to mount higher and higher. When the great man did appear he searched high and low for a *transformateur*. This apparatus is, apparently, necessary as the town voltage is 110 volts, and we in the country have a voltage of 220. When he found it it was very hot and in a few hours would have been on fire. Things one does not understand can be terrifying, and I haven't even the most elementary knowledge of electricity, though since very nearly losing my life through an electrical device I have a very wholesome respect and fear of its invisible power.

My Russian put a battery charger in my garage, which is situated at the top of the garden, opening on to the road — about a hundred yards from the house. He then most amiably proceeded to charge the battery of my car on his own responsibility. He had put the charger on a shelf with two long wires emerging from it to be attached to the battery. Having charged it to his satisfaction he detached the wires, leaving them sticking out into the air and, being a vague Russian, forgot to disconnect the charger, which he left alive.

It was a dark winter evening and I suddenly remembered that we needed some commodity in the town, so decided to jump into *Desirée*, my first Fiat car, and go and fetch it. I backed her into the road and did not trouble to tell my Margharita that I was going out; for she was busy in the kitchen preparing supper, and the little journey would take me only half an hour. I accomplished it satisfactorily, returned, opened the garage, and drove in. I did not bother to turn on the light, for I knew every corner of the garage by heart, so got out of the car and threw a rug over the bonnet.

As I did so I was touched by something and, putting out my hand, seized the two waving live wires attached to the charger.

A frightful terrifying sensation as I received the full force of 220 volts and found that those awful wires WOULD NOT LET ME GO! I seemed to be in the horrible grip of some superhuman monster. I shall never forget that awful feeling of being held by an invisible Power.

One thinks quickly at such times. I realised that I could never make Margharita, far below in the kitchen of my solid-built stone house, hear me if I cried for help. I also realised that she had the key to the *cabanon* next door to the garage, where the main electric switch is housed. This, I thought, is the end; for the gardener had gone home, we live on a lonely little mountain, and I knew that I could not long survive this terrible sensation which was already clouding my senses.

Then Someone seemed to take charge, far more powerful than that diabolic danger, and gave a last gleam of intelligence to my dizzy brain. Those wires must be attached to some plug in the wall that gave them life.

"With your free hand FIND THE PLUG AND PULL IT OUT! ACT QUICKLY!" said an Inner Voice.

Staggering forward I fumbled along the wall with my left hand, found the plug, and pulled it out. Then with what strength I had left I opened the door into the garden, and wrapping my burnt hand in the folds of my coat I ran drunkenly down the long garden stairway and burst into the kitchen.

"Margharita! Have you washed up the tea things?"

She looked at me reproachfully, for it was unlike her *Madame* to make such a tempestuous entrance and seem to hustle her. She explained with hurt dignity that she had not yet had time. They were still in the service lift and would be washed up with the supper things later on, but first she must prepare my vegetable soup.

Opening the door of the service lift I seized the teapot, took out a handful of tea-leaves, and clamped them upon my blackened palm. The tannic acid saved me from blistering, but even so I had a useless hand in a sling for many weeks. Since then I am always terrified that *any* electrical apparatus will bite me; only lately I had a lovely safety-apparatus fixed on the wall outside my bedroom, and now all I have to do to silence too-talkative bells and cut the electric current completely in case of a violent thunderstorm is to press down a little handle and immediately the whole house is plunged in darkness. The electrician who placed it even assured me that if any trouble occurred on the main line my little machine will cut off the current automatically all by his little self. Clever little machine — IF he does it! I haven't much faith in French-made devices.

But I do advise anyone building a house anywhere, certainly lone ignorant women like me, especially in Provence, not to be *too* artistic about their plumbing and electric wiring, especially if their house be built of stone. Hidden pipes and tubes are all very well, but plumbers and electricians are apt to die or leave the neighbourhood or a war intervenes and the owner of that house is completely lost. When I came back here in

1945 I suffered much from the complete ignorance of the whereabouts of all my installations, and when a water-leak occurred and must be discovered somewhere inside the house or garden walls, masons and plumbers were obliged to knock holes in them, and Henri, then a newcomer, to dig for the pipes and traps in the garden. In the end it was he who found the leak, but my little *Domaine* looked as though shaken up by an earthquake. However we do know now where our pipes are to be found.

The same Russian electrician wired the enormous house of another of my absentee neighbours. The owner had thrown many cottages into one, and when building a tower and two loggias, an extra wing and other additions, including five bathrooms, he had nevertheless taken care to roof the place with ancient "split-drain-pipe" Provençal tiles and to insist that the slope of the roofs be gentle and picturesque. Picturesque they certainly are, but the slope of them is so gentle that rain sits in puddles upon them, filters through ceilings, and soaks into the porous stone walls, so that in wet weather they are completely alive with electricity and anyone touching them anywhere gets a shock. Bells cannot be rung for the same reason, and anyone taking a bath at night must have it by candle-light or be electrocuted.

The house, which could be so lovely, has lain empty and derelict for nearly two years. Thieves have entered and stolen nearly all its equipment, and the garden is a jungle of weeds. The pity of it! But no English person would now be allowed to take out the thousands of francs necessary to reroof the place and put in a new electric installation which, in France to-day, would cost millions of francs. I, who remember that house in its glory, am saddened by its condition to-day.

The furniture of all the houses on this mountain, save mine, has changed places many times. If I make the acquaintance of tenants in one of them I am sure to see chairs or mats or table equipment borrowed from another house once so familiar to me. Our peasant friends, engaged to look after tenants, have no hesitation in borrowing anything lacking in the house where they are temporarily working, for at one time we English on this mountain were like one happy family. Now no one remembers what belongs where.

I gave a dinner-party and engaged Francis, a dear man, an old friend and an excellent *Maître d'Hôtel*, who was always engaged to help at all our parties and still comes to me. My numbers increased at the last moment. The telephone bell rings:

"Darling, I fear I can't come to-night because my brother has flown out unexpectedly to see me and you'll understand that I can't leave him alone on his first night."

"Oh! can't you bring him too — and another woman to balance him?" I reply.

"Oh, *may* I? How lovely!"

Hurriedly I inform Francis that we shall have two extra guests and he must somehow seat them. When I come downstairs I find that he has obeyed me and one of my tables has two familiar chairs placed beside it — but not MY chairs — ! I ask no questions, but Francis knows that I have an inflamed conscience about borrowing the possessions of others in their absence, and I notice with relief that in the morning those two extra chairs have disappeared. I, in my turn, supplement tenanted houses with silver, glass, crockery and cutlery, for during a war of five years this form of equipment gets broken or stolen, and only now can one buy replacements — at a terrific cost. English absentee landlords cannot get out money to buy these things for their houses, but tenants occupying them naturally expect to be able to entertain guests in this lovely spot, and are indignant when they find only the bare necessities for a very small household. I, who have been lucky enough to have my possessions guarded by a faithful friend and my house kept in perfect condition by a devoted *bonne*, am glad to be able to supplement things lacking in the houses once so familiar to me and owned by loved friends long since dead. For their honour I do it.

CHAPTER TWO

The Water-Guard

Le Gardien des Eaux

We who live in the South of France are always preoccupied with the problem of water — or rather the lack of it. The wise buyer of land there should first inquire how many concessions of water go with it, and whether these are for *ménage* (household) or *irrigation* (gardens). One concession of water is always given — a mere trickle — enough to mix the mortar for building or repairing a house; but many more are required if the owner desires a bath or to put his land into cultivation.

In every district there is a Water-Guard, and his business is to direct concessions to various habitations down pipes leading from great reservoirs in the mountains.

This Man of Pipes, it will at once be realised, is a Power in the land. Alas! he is seldom incorruptible. We sometimes find that our water has ceased to flow, and can be pretty sure that our neighbour, *Monsieur* X., having need of extra water for his *jasmin* terraces during the great heat, has suborned the Water-Guard to divert the flow of other people's concessions into his own reservoir. These irate people then follow the usual procedure of writing their complaints and pushing the notes into a box provided for that purpose on the main road. But it seems that only notes of another variety will cause the Man of Pipes to make that precious fluid flow once more in the right direction; for he opens that box but once a year.

It will be realised that this Position of Power can be lucrative if its occupant possesses a personality strong enough to impress his victims. If *Monsieur* Y. is in urgent need of water he may perhaps out-bribe the lawful owner, who has himself been blackmailed into paying a sum to regain his stolen fluid, and so the game can go on indefinitely.

I am one of the few who have had the courage to stand up for their rights. I have what my husband called "a raging sense of equity," and since I came to Provence I have firmly refused to bribe the Water-Guard to give me what is mine by right. I will not be intimidated by the ferocious mien of that huge swarthy Corsican. Once I walked the three kilometres to beard him in his den, a small stone cottage set amid vines above the main road. He was working in his vineyard, and when he saw me coming he at once began to shout very rude remarks about people who neglected to keep down brambles near the fount of their water-supply, so that no human being could possibly be expected to turn on the concessions. He continued to bawl and to bluster as I drew nearer.

I had said no word, but his guilty conscience no doubt warned him that I had come to complain of lack of water. I smiled amiably and promised that my gardener should immediately clear away those non-existent brambles, and that thenceforth I should expect to be given my full ration of water.

As I turned away I told him that we English might be considered "*têtes dûres*," but if we were wooden-headed we were not fools, were straight in our dealings and not unreasonable: if we paid for something we expected to get it. I bade him farewell, and to the accompaniment of growls and impolite remarks which, perhaps fortunately, were soon inaudible, I trudged homeward.

Next day water flowed once more into my depleted reservoirs, and for a time I had no cause for complaint.

That summer my neighbour, "*Mademoiselle*" of the *Château* below, suggested that we should go up to our *Bergerie* in the High Alps to escape the heat. Neither of us could stand *la grande chaleur* of July and August, but always we left our gardens with much apprehension; for unless they are watered regularly and well, both before sunrise and after sundown, gardens here become parched immediately, and tender young vegetables and flowers wither away. Then very often the banks of the gigantic reservoir that feeds the little towns and villages need repair, and our water-supply may be cut, sometimes for two days, and we must decide which plants vitally need water from our reserve *bassins* and which can survive for another day. Few Provençal gardeners have any initiative, and it is usually *Monsieur* or *Madame* who must decide these problems.

However, risks must sometimes be taken and off we went, after leaving detailed instructions to meet, as we hoped, any eventuality.

Peacefully we installed ourselves in our eagle's nest; and, during the glorious weeks that followed, we picked armfuls of pheasant-eye narcissus, lay in full sunshine upon the gentian-starred plateau; plunged, daily, for a breath-taking icy moment into the little mountain torrent that bordered the property, then ran races with the dogs, all entering the *Bergerie* hungrily afterwards to devour delicacies cooked by the expert *Mademoiselle*. Then I woke up one morning with uncomfortable presentiments.

"I have an awful certainty that all is not well at home," I announced to *Mademoiselle* while making our morning coffee.

She rolled a dark eye at me full of distaste.

"What an announcement to make before we've even had our *petit déjeuner*!" she growled.

"I feel sure that awful Water-Guard has cut off the water-supply," I went on relentlessly. "My poor garden!"

"But you left stamped and addressed postcards to be sent to you in case of any emergency, and there's been the most heavenly silence and peace since we came here — and now *you* are doing your best to spoil it with your fussing," expostulated *Mademoiselle. "Really!"*

I drank the coffee in gloomy silence, feeling every moment more strongly that my presence was sorely needed at home; while she, with an apprehensive glance at me, for in the past she had suffered much from my presentiments of imminent disaster (both great and small) which hitherto had been only too well founded, seized her coffee-cup and buttered roll and swung out into the sunshine, to sit by the edge of our plateau gazing at the Meije glacier — far from my depressing company. All day I strove to be gay and natural; but have you not noticed that if you strive to be anything the result is generally complete failure? Anyway my efforts evidently lacked sincerity and spontaneity; for during the afternoon, instead of taking a canvas out-of-doors and sketching, *Mademoiselle* suddenly hauled down her knapsack from the beam where it swung and began hurling various possessions upon her shepherd's bed.

"You'd better pack, too," she said to me savagely, "for I see that we shall have no more peace or happiness while you're under this cloud of apprehension. Well, we'll go home if only to assure you that everything's all right. We shall just have to bear that tiresome drive back to the *Midi*, grill there for a day or two, and then return having spent hundreds of francs on petrol and shortened the life of the tyres."

Feeling very guilty I, also, hauled down my knapsack and began, silently, to pack. It seemed selfish to drag *Mademoiselle* from that Paradise of flowers, and from the life-giving freshness of air that blew straight from the glaciers around us, just because I had that uncomfortable feeling in my bones that something had gone wrong at home. I would have gone back by myself, but it would be unsafe to leave her alone on that isolated peak, and she always imagined that some catastrophe would happen to me on the road. So there it was, and the long drive must be endured together.

We made it successfully, though as we approached the south we and the dogs panted and gasped for air. It was impossible to touch the metal-work of the car without risk of blistering, and even the accelerator burned through one's sandals. *Mademoiselle* turned a mocking eye on me as with a stifled exclamation I discovered this when I took my turn at the wheel.

"Are you beginning to regret the *Bergerie*?" she murmured, with that slow smile of hers which could disarm any irony.

"We shall enjoy it all the more when we get back; having put right whatever it is that has gone wrong," I retorted stubbornly. I halted the car, removed my sandal, and bound a handkerchief round my bare foot; then replaced the sandal — thonged leather Phœnician footwear such as is still made by the little cobbler of St Tropez.

Something *had* gone wrong, and if I had not returned to set it right it would have cost me many thousand francs which I could ill afford. I found my two open *bassins*, each built to hold, when filled as they should have been, twenty thousand litres of water, quite dry. The gardener, an unlettered peasant (as I should have realised before giving him post-cards to send to me) wringing his hands, led me up to the garage and pointed to the gauge that informs us of the amount of water in my largest reservoir (fifty thousand litres) under the roof of the garage. The tell-tale lump of lead was right up at the top of the gauge. All too plainly this *bassin* also was dry.

Those who live in Provence will realise the vital importance of keeping *bassins* filled lest the hot sun crack the cement and render them useless. Even when repaired they are ever after liable to leak at the weakened place when the water suffers changes of temperature. Reservoirs are enormously expensive to build and I am not a rich woman. When *Mademoiselle* saw my dry *bassins* she was horrified, and admitted that once more my "presentiments" had been justified.

I ignored the usual procedure, certain that the "complaint-box" must be as full as my *bassins* were empty, and I was too angry with the Water-Guard to seek him out: this time he should come to me — at once.

Knowing his habits I telephoned to the little Café-Bar, near his habitation, where he invariably takes his apéritif at noon, and left an urgent message to say that I had returned from the High Alps and must see him immediately.

I rather wondered then what I should do if he defied me; for his usual routine is to pay ceremonial visits and turn taps in the mornings and take a siesta in the afternoons. But on this occasion his conscience — I suppose he must have a faint wriggle inside which sometimes makes him feel uncomfortable — was so clouded with sins of omission and commission that he arrived soon after *déjeuner* when the sun was at its hottest. I heard him from afar, blustering and growling as is his wont, and from an upper window saw his tall gaunt form loping down the mountain road leading to my *Domaine*. I went downstairs and stood in the courtyard beside the empty *bassin* near the house awaiting him.

Following his usual tactics he attacked me at once.

Why were my *bassins* empty? What inexcusable carelessness! Did I not know, after living so long in this country, that if *bassins* were left empty under a hot sun they cracked and were ruined for ever?

He whirled his arms like flails as he bawled his reproaches at me.

I waited until he had perforce to pause to regain breath, and then asked him WHY he had turned off the water in my absence. It was his duty to see that my *bassins* were kept filled with water, for which I paid large sums.

Why had I not complained before, he raved.

Because I was up in the High Alps (as he very well knew) and I had trusted the Water-Guard to do no more than his duty.

I must get a plumber, he yelled; no doubt my supply-pipe was blocked by a frog or a fish.

I told him gently that I would at once visit the High Authorities of the Water Board in our largest town and ask *them* to investigate my supply pipe and remove the obstructing frog or fish and to place a filter at its opening to prevent such an accident happening again.

He saw, I am certain, the mocking light in my eye — did I detect one in his? — for he knew full well that I knew why my *bassins* were empty. I think he must also have sensed my sneaking admiration for his consummate cheek. Anyhow, as he turned to go he gave me a quick sidelong look from those smouldering eyes, and the ghost of a grin twisted that bitter mouth.

"I will report that fish — or frog — to Headquarters this afternoon," I promised him in farewell; for I never make an official complaint without first warning the offender of my intention.

I was as good as my word. Hot as it was I got out the car and drove the eight *kilometres* to the town. The H.Q. staff of the Water Board were visibly melting in their stuffy little office. As the Director was invisible I made my complaint to the Head Clerk.

He listened to the story, then grinned gently, tapped his nose, and remarked —

"*Ah! c'est un brigand, lui!*" (so they *knew* he was a *brigand* and allowed him to go on with his *brigandage*).

"*C'est un Corse!*" I replied satirically (for we know that Corsica is said to abound in brigands).

To my intense consternation a dark head reared above the glass partition which ensures the *Directeur* some measure of privacy, and a furious voice spat at me these words —

"*Moi aussi! Moi je suis Corse, Madame!*" I had unwittingly insulted the very man whose aid and support I had come to seek! Usually I have only what the French describe as "*l'esprit de l'escalier,*" staircase wit, and think, as I go downstairs after an interview, of all the telling things and fine phrases that I *might* have used. But on this occasion sudden inspiration came, and, with a little bow and my sweetest smile, I replied in a flash —

"*Ah, Monsieur, le Grand Napoléon aussi était Corse. Il-y-a toujours des exceptions.*"

The enraged face broke into a smile, and an appreciative chuckle ran round the office. As I was bowed out by the Director himself I felt that, after all, my visit might not prove fruitless.

During the early hours of that airless night, lying sleepless upon my bed, I suddenly heard the loveliest sound, the splash of water below my window. Gazing out into brilliant moonlight I saw a black ever-widening stain upon the white floor of my *bassin*. A moonbeam caught the source of it, a glorious jet of water — far more than my ration surely — flowing into it in a silver stream. It was a truly wonderful sight, and one that I had not dared hope to see for many days, because this smaller *bassin* is fed by the overflow from the other two, so that I knew at once that they must be already brimming over.

H.Q. Water Supply had done their work well and quickly, and I wondered how many concessions of how many people were now pouring into my *bassin*; then consoled myself with the thought that, after all, mine must have been feeding theirs for some long time while my garden suffered. Anyhow, I felt it to be something of a triumph that a quick repartee had achieved what others had only gained by crossing the horny palm of a Corsican with silver — or more probably notes.

Mademoiselle and I returned to our cool Alpine retreat, and when we came back at the end of the summer we were assured that water had flowed regularly down our pipes. Nevertheless I knew that my direct action had not endeared me to the Man of Pipes. My *bonne* told me that she thought his temper had been soured by the desertion of his wife, who had left him for another man with whom she lived in the same village, so that the deserted husband, who was also saddled with the young child, had no chance of forgetting or forgiving her infidelity. *Not* a tactful woman.

This story somewhat softened my opinion of the poor man, though I felt it to be unfair that he should vent his spleen upon innocent people like myself and my friends.

Then war broke upon us, and when I returned to Provence in 1945 I found that many changes had taken place. But our water-supply was still in charge of the Corsican brigand!

There had been a drought for three years and nearly all the vegetation had died; there was no pasturage for beasts and they had therefore been killed and eaten. The Water-Guards of every district were strictly enjoined to give only enough of the rare and precious water to keep the bases of reservoirs covered, and a trickle of water for each house just to keep its inhabitants alive.

I worked hard that first winter distributing to the children of Provence the clothes and comforts I had collected from generous people at home; and I became *Marraine* of forty orphans of men of the Resistance, brought to me bare-footed and in rags. One morning I read in the local newspaper that a small boy in a neighbouring village had, of his own accord, taken his old toys, treasured since before the war, and presented them all to my orphan *fllleuls*. Deeply touched, I telephoned to a woman I knew in that village and asked her to tell the little boy to come to me at *Domaine de Fort Escu*, where there was a parcel waiting for him.

That very afternoon the bell outside my courtyard gate rang loudly. I was sorting clothes in the loggia nearby and ran to open it. Standing outside was — the

Water-Guard holding proudly by the hand a small blond boy! It was this child who had given up his toys to my orphans, and now Papa had brought him to fetch the parcel promised by *Madame*.

I led them into the loggia and there heard a pathetic story. The Water-Guard, his lantern-jawed face transfigured with tenderness as he looked at his small son, told me of the hard struggle it had been to be father and mother in one to his *gosse*. The child was scrupulously clean, and his clothes, though scanty, had been patched and darned with dragon's-teeth stitches by Papa, who also did the cooking and all the cleaning of the house. His dark eyes, which hitherto I had seldom seen except when they were smouldering with fury, glowed with love and pride as he looked at his little son. *Could* this be the gigantic ogre who had bullied us and tyrannised over us all for so many years!

I began to look through what clothes remained. The child had none but those he wore — nothing at all for *le Dimanche*, and this he felt cruelly when he went to Mass on Sunday.

I found some shorts and a tweed coat which fitted fairly well. But what to wear under the coat? Hesitatingly I produced a very smart white flannel waistcoat with the initials R. B. embroidered inside a shield in dark blue, evidently part of some school sports uniform and very nearly new.

I held it up saying that this was all that I had left, but unfortunately these initials . . .

"Your surname begins with B.," I said, "but the R.?"

"Son petit nom est RÉNÉ!" bawled the father in his familiar stentorian voice. Then, throwing back his head and roaring with laughter, he slapped his thighs and pivoted on his heels, shouting —

"R. B.! R. B.! R. B.! *Quelle chance! Quelle coincidence!"*

What further delighted him was that his son's initials were enclosed in a shield exactly like the one fixed to my gateway bearing the legend *"Domaine de Fort Escu."* This was a sign from *le bon Dieu* that *Madame* must be Réné's *Marraine.*

Well, why not? I had already been adopted as *Marraine* by three hundred men of the French Heavy Artillery in 1939. In England I had collected many lonely *poilus*, and lately had been added unto me these forty orphans of the Resistance. Why not a little boy, half Corsican and half French, who, oddly enough, looked completely English with his blond head and blue eyes. His fair skin now flushed pink with excitement as I tried on that white waistcoat which, *Dieu merci!* fitted perfectly.

Father and son walked off hand in hand, radiant and proud, each with a fat parcel under his arm, one of them containing precious American *bon-bons* for Réné. I watched them moving down the road — the very tall man and the small boy — and waved to them in farewell.

"R. B.! R. B.!" yelled the Man of Pipes to me over his shoulder, and banged his boy joyously with the parcel . . .

Since when my water-supply has never failed.

CHAPTER
THREE

The Compleat Gardener

I must now introduce Henri, my gardener. For four years now he has had complete control of my property — and, I fear, of me. For since I came back here I have been unable to plant my flowers and puddle happily in my garden. First the children of Provence occupied my time entirely. Then I had to undergo a major operation; and now a dilated heart stops my joyous activities, and therefore Henri has complete sway in my *Domaine*.

In Provence we have various types of gardeners, neatly classified by the C.G.T. (the French equivalent of our English Trades Union). Once upon a time a gardener was just a gardener with more — or less — experience. Now we have *Category A.*, the man who understands the cultivation of hot-house flowers and can prune all manner of fruit trees, roses and shrubs, in addition to the more ordinary work of a gardener. *Category B.*, the man who only occupies himself with vegetables and flowers; *Category C.*, just a peasant who digs and tidies up.

Their wages are regulated by the C.G.T. and graded according to their capabilities, also their various insurances.

The French apparently love to grade. You can have a funeral of *Première Classe* with plumes and mutes, a magnificent hearse and the most expensive coffin; or one of *Deuxième Classe* without plumes and grandeur but still making somewhat of a show; or, for *Troisième Classe*, you can just be trundled along on a little black-and-white bier by your friends, which, to me, is far more cosy.

But this is my usual irrelevance, for we were speaking of gardeners and not of personal planting.

My present gardener is a naïve and lovable villain with the widest smile — which NEVER comes off — and the widest stern I have ever seen on a human being, and as he is constantly potting, weeding and bending I see a great deal of it. Its proportions are accentuated by an oblong patch (set horizontally) of dark-blue cotton upon a background of faded blue trousers. This is a war-decoration, for it was impossible to get matching material, and decency sometimes demanded a harlequin effect. When I first came back in 1945 I saw some lovely and variegated effects of colour when the whole population was picking up olives and the countryside was peppered with *derrières*. One recognised one's peasant neighbours by their patches.

Henri is in *Category A*. This may sound very grand for a woman with an extremely precarious income, earned by a pen which is sometimes paralysed for long periods by ill-health, but Henri is an elastic *Category A.* and really earns the enormous wages I have to give him. He does anything and everything — and I am pretty sure "does" me — but I am conveniently blind, because he is

so useful and I consider that his happy grin, which
NOTHING, not rain, hail, snow, ravaging mistral nor
burning scirocco can wash, freeze, blow or scorch away,
is beyond price.

He came to me in this-wise.

On my return here I found the whole of my property
completely neglected and overgrown, save for a few
terraces of vegetables which my faithful *bonne*,
Margharita, had cultivated to provide food for herself.
She had sedulously watered my dwarf English roses
because she knew how much I love them, but the
ramblers were beyond her power to succour, and far
beyond her reach, even had she known how to prune
them, and they had raced up a twenty-foot wall, down
over the other side and across the lane, to the great
discomfort of passing peasants whose already ragged
trousers were torn by thorns.

My cypress trees were bewhiskered, and they, too,
had shot up so high that it was impossible, without a
tall ladder, to remove the clusters of cones which
weighed down the side branches and make them neat
and clean-shaven again. The bignonia and wistaria had
clambered all over the house, making it quite impossible
to open the shutters which had remained closed over the
windows for so long.

The garden looked lovely but extremely unkempt, like
the garden of *La Belle au Bois Dormant* must have
looked, and obviously something must be done about it
— How on earth could I pay the small army of men that
would be needed to prune the roses, trim the cypresses,

renew the soil in my cold frames, and do all that must be done to put the place in order?

As I puzzled over this problem, suddenly I thought of my poor *Desirée*, my much-loved Fiat car which had been trussed up on blocks in a garage deserted since the death of my *Mademoiselle*. The tenant of my house had needed the garage for *her* car, and I had left *Desirée* with *Mademoiselle* to do ambulance work for the French troops when I left France in 1940. She was a big saloon car, and I had caused the backs of her front seats to be made to descend so that *Mademoiselle* and I could sleep in her when we toured France and Italy. After *Mademoiselle's* death she was left unprotected, and her five beautiful tyres were stolen by Italians, Germans, or perhaps some dishonest person who could make 45,000 francs per tyre.

Her carcase was of no use to me; for even if I could have procured tyres from England, her engine consumed far too much petrol, which was then almost as rare and expensive as tyres.

I decided to sell her chassis and with the money to hire a band of gardeners from a leading horticulturist in Grasse to make my garden lovely again.

This I did, and the little army of gardeners appeared one day led by — Henri! I had known him slightly for years; for pruning roses and fruit trees was beyond the powers of our dear old Hilaire (who would now be classed as *Category B*. and has, bless his faithful bald head, long been planted in the earth he tended so lovingly). We had appealed to our famous *Horticulteur*, and he sent us Henri, his head man, for a day.

One day sounds inadequate to do all the pruning necessary, but Henri is a tiger for work (*when* he works) and accomplishes more in a day than other gardeners achieve in a week. He is of Herculean proportions, and even at the hungry moment of which I write, could never have been described as under-nourished. His skin is oily and of a ruddy brown, his eyes clear, blue and laughing, and except after visits to the *coiffeur*, his mop of curly chestnut curls are full of light and vigour and always standing on end. Daily his face resembles more and more a full moon, and steadily he puts on weight. So heavy is he that when he was standing upon a stone seat the better to prune a luxuriant shrub which shadowed it, I saw that stone seat crack in half. On another occasion, when he was thudding with the *"dame,"* a circular piece of iron attached to a long handle with which gardeners flatten the surface of roads or lawns, there was a sudden landslide and the supporting wall of huge boulders rolled down to the terrace below and half my newly-planted lawn, sown with *le gazon permanent du Midi*, with it. Once when I asked Henri if he was dancing with his wife at a local *fête*, he shook his head, smiling of course, and replied:

"Non, Madame. Moi je suis trop éléphant."

An elephant he is, and when I see him climbing my trees and balancing precariously upon branches as he prunes them, I wonder how anything so enormous and so heavy can perform such extraordinary feats of balance and agility or how my trees support his weight.

But I anticipate the installation of Henri in my little *Domaine* and must explain now how he came to be in my service.

He arrived with his army of gardeners, and after a preliminary glance around the property, each step punctuated by *"Ah! là-là!"* and laughing blue eyes rolled heavenwards, they set to work. In a week the cypress trees were shorn and pointed, the cypress hedges smooth walls of verdure; the rambler roses were curbed and trained, and the soil renewed in the frames. Once more it was possible to open the *persiennes* and to let in light into my darkened rooms; bonfires of burning rubbish and clipped greenery blazed in hidden corners. My garden was once more as it had been, but more beautiful because of the luxuriant growth of five years.

Always I noticed with approval that, although he was foreman, Henri took upon himself the heaviest labour and worked *with* his men instead of merely directing them. One day, when he was controlling the wild growth of a rampant climbing rose, clipping here with seccateurs, nailing up a trailing branch of young growth so that in flowering time *Madame* could see *guirlandes de roses* from her bedroom window — a lovely sight — I perched on the wall above him, and marvelling at the skill and dexterity of his great fingers, told him that I thought his job was the most beautiful of all professions.

Quickly he contradicted me, saying that in his case it was a sad and tantalising one, for he never saw the results of his work. He was sent here and there to prune and to plant, but whether his labour proved successful he never knew. He confided to me his secret ambition — one day to have in his charge a small property where he could sow seeds, transplant, bed out, and then watch the glory of flowering; prune fruit trees and see them laden with peaches, plums, pears, and apricots. This I could so well understand. He had spoken with complete sincerity as he looked wistfully around him at the fruit trees he had pruned so carefully and the climbing roses on my walls. I resolved when the fruiting and flowering season was over that I would write a report of the results of their work to Henri and his workmen. And I said:

"Henri, if you are serious and ever do contemplate taking a small private place, think of me — for I need someone like you to work here."

He told me that his wages were terribly high, and I told him that if he ever came to me he would have to be ready to do every kind of job in addition to his garden work. He would be responsible for the central heating in winter, he must chop wood, he must run errands, he must help me to drag heavy cases of clothes and comforts for my Relief work, pump up the tyres of my little Grey Pigeon (my gallant little Baby Austin); in fact do anything and everything, but never, NEVER could I afford to give him extra help.

"You have always had men to work under you, Henri," I said, "and you must understand that I should never be able to afford even *one* under-gardener. You would have to dig and plant, prune and spray the vines unaided."

He assured me that he would be prepared to do this. After all it was just *la vie*.

Life, yes, but a pretty hard life even if varied.

We had a wonderful fruit and flower season that year thanks to Henri and his men — and, of course, *le bon Dieu* — and I wrote a detailed report of the state of my garden and the results of their so successful efforts, addressing it to Henri with a request that it should be read to his helpers. In reply he told me that never before had he received such a letter and that he and the under-gardeners were so grateful to me for writing it. This missive was signed by them all, beautified for me by a few muddy finger-prints.

Three or four months later I was driving into Grasse when I saw Henri pedalling furiously along on his bicycle, curls on end as usual. When he saw me his smile widened from ear to ear, and with that incredible agility so incongruous in an 'elephant,' he manœuvred his bicycle to my car, sprang off it, and stood red and beaming beside it.

"I was coming to see *Madame*," he said, "to ask her if she was serious when she said she would like me to work for her. I gave notice to the *horticulteur* this morning and already I have been offered another place. But I promised *Madame* to give her *la préférence*."

What joy to have an experienced man to tend my loved garden! His wages scared me to death, but I reflected that *if* he was willing to undertake *all* the work of my *Domaine* single-handed it would hardly be more costly than having a *Category B.* gardener and getting in experts to do all the varieties of pruning.

Once more I repeated my conditions, and as each was stated he nodded vigorously. He *wanted* to come to me — and come he did.

Since then each member of my small household has piled her troubles upon Henri, sure of swift aid and that encouraging smile. He bicycles daily from Grasse in all weathers and my *bonne* gives him endless commissions to do for her — she has forgotten to get butter, she lacks this and that, and Henri brings it. He posts letters for me and buys stamps; he climbs into the *grenier* to get down suitcases and trunks; he empties my huge Venetian jar, cleans and refills it so that *Madame* can arrange fresh flowers therein; and after my gall-bladder was removed in 1947 it was Henri who said that now he would be *le bâton de Madame* and he acted as her support when she first could totter around her beloved garden. Streaming with sweat he shyly offered his damp arm, and, beaming with pride, showed her each flower that he had planted and all the succulent young vegetables ready for her eating. I exhausted my adjectives of praise.

When the difficult moment came and I was obliged — somehow — to climb the five steep steps leading to my Studio he very nearly finished me. Standing behind me he begged me to have complete confidence in him. Putting one huge hand under each of my armpits so that my arms were raised nearly above my head and my hands therefore powerless to support my poor split tumpkin, he then, with all his great strength, positively *rushed* me up those steps and flumped me, completely breathless with shock and laughter, upon my divan near the door. Never was made a more undignified ascent, and why he didn't burst all those stitches I do not know. For some hours, afterwards my pulse raced at 120 to the minute.

The next time I went out I waited till after *Midi*, when Henri was eating his *déjeuner* inside his *cabanon* (with a stove roaring to heat his food and the door and window closed on a stifling day in June) and then descended those steep steps on my *derrière* and later mounted them in the same manner — even less dignified but far safer, and only my pride was wounded, not the feelings of Henri.

Never has he asked for help in his work. True to his promise he performs prodigies of labour single-handed. One of the most maddening of his tasks is clipping the cypress hedges, because, if he is working alone, it is necessary for him constantly to descend from his ladder to see if he is keeping them level, then climb up again to continue his clipping. He is very patient and always good-tempered.

My English friends scattered about the neighbourhood are so impressed by Henri's expert work that they are apt to ask him the names of many of my shrubs and flowers. He is never at a loss and fills them up with completely fabulous information. The ignorant are suitably impressed, and Henri, flattered, beams, bows, and withdraws. On the faces of those friends who have some knowledge of horticulture I have sometimes seen an expression of doubt — even of amazement as when Henri was asked the name of that mauve and purple salvia, soft to the touch like chenille, he informed them with great assurance that it was a cotoneaster and then, to prove his words, asked the inquirers to stroke the flower and they would find that it was like *coton*.

I had found out early that Henri only knew the names of his adored *paquerettes*, those fat dwarf double daisies, pink or white, and of the pansies and marigolds with which he loves to 'bed out' the few strips of deep earth between outcrops of rock. But NEVER would he admit ignorance upon *any* subject. I have known him hesitate for an instant, snapping the middle finger and thumb of a hand raised heavenwards when I have suddenly asked him the name of a shrub (which I knew perfectly well), before glibly giving me erroneous information — and have been obliged to admire his complete self-assurance.

Visitors have found to their cost that when they have asked Henri the times when the *autobus* passes the end of my lane on its way from Nice to Grasse or vice versa, he will tell them the hours with the greatest emphasis. Believing him, they will sometimes wait by the side of the dusty main road for a very, very long time.

At one moment I thought that it would be extremely useful to have a little Peugeot *camionette* to take surplus vegetables to market, and I asked Henri if he could drive a car. He nodded vigorously and told me that he possessed a driving licence.

Accordingly I bought a little second-hand car, but when I suggested that he should drive into Grasse to get various things needed for the garden, to my consternation he rather sheepishly admitted to me that he had only once driven without an instructor by his side, and that was in the year 1935 . . ! He owned that he would be scared to drive the little Peugeot in case he damaged it. And I had bought it for his use! Having bought it I saw that *Madame* herself would be obliged to do those errands.

But Henri was not equally frank with the Gazelle when she came out from England last year to stay with me. She had her English driving licence, but had never driven in France, so I gave her a few lessons to accustom her to the French rules of the road, and especially to mountain tracks, hairpin-bends, and the mad reckless-ness of French drivers who cut in at corners, roar out of side-roads without warning, and do other dangerous deeds.

We had been picking up olives for weeks. Some had fallen prematurely, having been attacked by some beastly little worm, and then had to be picked up before the ripe fruit was ready. Then sheets of sacking would be laid under the tree and men (in my case only Henri) would climb up to *gauler les arbres* — beat the branches gently with bamboos to make the ripe fruits fall upon them, so saving much labour. We had all been at work and were suffering from back-ache — in the olive season every peasant complains of *mal aux reins* and, when standing, supports the small of his aching back with his two hands while engaged in conversation — and at last all the purple-black fallen fruit had been picked up. That evening Henri triumphantly announced that to-morrow he would knock down the remainder of the crop, for now he could spread his sheets. But — in the night rose up a terrific mistral. The wind howled round the house like a pack of wolves, doors were wrenched from their hinges if left open, garden chairs were whirled into the air and blown across the courtyard, tiles were lifted from the roof and sailed into neighbouring properties — and my olive-crop was blown from the trees and once more peppered the ground. All our back-breaking work was to be continued.

However all things eventually come to an end, and at last we cleared the terraces and filled many heavy sacks with the fruit which must now be transported to the olive-mill — in the little Peugeot *camionette* — to be crushed into precious oil.

As the sacks were too heavy for the Gazelle to lift, I suggested that Henri should accompany her in the Peugeot. Willingly he heaved first the sacks and then his own great bulk into the car and sat, beaming of course, proudly beside her.

The drive up to the mill from the valley is a little tricky; for the ascent is steep, one must turn a completely blind corner and possibly find a crowd of *camions* unloading sacks of olives before the entrance to the mill. In that event it is necessary to do complicated manœuvres to turn the car on a steep slope and in a limited space. I enjoined Henri to get out at the foot of the hill and walk ahead to warn my little *chauffeuse* of possible blocks and dangers around that blind corner, and then to direct her as she turned the car in the narrow *cul-de-sac*.

I repeated my instructions slowly and carefully because, having often delivered olives to the mill, I knew the difficulties and dangers and had never exactly enjoyed the adventure. It would be good experience for the child, and the presence of Henri, directing operations, would give her assurance and rob the expedition of possible danger. Henri nodded vigorously and begged *Madame* not to torment herself because HE would protect *Mademoiselle* and guide her to her goal.

Tranquilly I returned to my Studio and my writing.

I should have felt far from tranquil had I known what was happening. At luncheon my little friend described her experiences. She admitted that the solid presence of Henri by her side *did* give her confidence, especially when she asked him if he could drive, and with a superior smile he assured her that he could. At intervals he bawled to her instructions and advice, ordering her to "*Klaxonnez! klaxonnez!*" at every bend of the road. Good advice in itself, for one can't sound one's horn often enough on these twisting mountain roads, but evidence, had she known that he had never driven alone, of slight nervousness.

When they approached the mill, Henri still remained by her side, urging her to accelerate as they ascended the hill. As he did not follow my implicit instructions to get out of the car and direct her movements, she happily was unaware of possible perils ahead and blithely rounded that blind corner with her heavy load (Henri and many sacks of olives) — to confront two huge *camions* completely blocking both the turning place and the entrance to the mill. The brakes of a second-hand car are seldom very strong and mine were — a bit odd. When applied they didn't hold, and if stopped upon a slope the car was liable to slip backwards, a really horrible sensation if there is a car behind you.

I gathered that all this happened, but I shall never know how that child came through the adventure safely, delivered her olives, and turned the car. A great achievement, but she told me that the presence of *so experienced a driver as Henri* had given her confidence — ! He had confessed his inexperience to me in fear that I should expect him to drive the car, but never would he admit ignorance to a young and pretty girl.

When I told her that Henri had never taken the wheel since 1935 and then only with an instructor beside him, her jaw dropped and she stared at me in consternation and amazement; then, having a delicious sense of humour, she burst into uncontrollable laughter.

"Oh, the CHEEK of him," she gasped, "the consummate cheek! And I believed his boasting and had complete confidence in him!"

I had confidence in Henri for a long time. Sometimes I used to wonder at the huge appetite of the rabbits he kept in his hutches in Grasse, for every day he bicycled home in the evening with a gigantic bundle packed carefully in sacking which he informed my elevated eyebrows contained *mauvaises herbes* which he had weeded from my terraces to nourish his *lapins*. Still believing this fable I wondered nevertheless how Henri and his wife, who have no family, could ceaselessly devour so many rabbits, for when one day I asked him if he bred and sold them — hoping to buy one for my household as my *bonne* had forgotten to order the meat — he told me that he never sold any, they were entirely for home consumption.

Gradually the seeds of distrust were sown in my mind by various peasant neighbours, by nods and winks and knowing smiles as they, the under-nourished, jerked thumbs in the direction of my enormous Henri who seems to put on more flesh daily and to exude more oil. What luck some people had, to be placed in full control of a property such as *Madame's*! What perquisites! One would never lack wine or olive oil with such abundance around one! And the vegetables! With such a quantity no one would miss a basketful daily — it could be carried home without risk of damage carefully packed in a *ballot* and transported on the carrier of a bicycle. These could not only be eaten at home, but could also be sold at a very high price in Grasse — and so on.

DID those enormous bundles contain hidden baskets of my vegetables carefully enveloped by weeds and greenery for Henri's rabbits? I began to wonder very uncomfortably, and one day I told Henri that it was high time he began to sell the surplus vegetables to help defray the heavy expenses of my garden; manure, spraying mixtures, tools, &c., and his very high wages. Sadly smiling, he shook his head as he assured me that at that fruitful moment the market was so overstocked with vegetables that we should get very poor prices, which would hardly cover the cost of transport, petrol being so expensive.

The very next day I suddenly decided to visit a friend in Grasse, and my departure in the car by chance coincided with that of Henri on his bicycle. Seeing me he looked thoroughly startled. Even his ears flushed red, for on the back of his bicycle was a truly enormous *ballot* — of rabbit fodder? Raising a huge hand in salutation he shot past me at a dangerous speed down the rocky track. I started up the car and followed behind.

49

Knowing that I must overtake him he decided to risk a short-cut through the olive grove ahead, across a track made by the French Army in 1939 to cut off a sharp corner, but long since made impossible for cars by the peasant who owned the land and who laboriously dug a trench across it. Henri, striving to keep ahead of "*Madame*-with-the-all-seeing-eye" — shot bravely at the trench and bumped and crashed across it. By a miracle he succeeded in keeping his seat; but the shock proved too much for his bundle, which came unmoored and rolled to the ground. Fortunately for him it was securely tied up and the contents remained unrevealed, but never before have I seen so embarrassed a man as I drove past him.

On the way to Grasse I upbraided myself for moral cowardice. I should have stopped the car and gone up to Henri and asked him to open his *ballot* and show its contents. What moral cowards most of us are! I am fond of Henri and I dreaded shaming him — and so I drove on leaving him unchallenged.

But I might have known that he would have a glib answer ready. The next day I met him in the garden. Smiling all over his face he tiptoed towards me ingratiatingly, waving a grubby scrap of paper and exclaiming exultantly:

"*J'ai vendu des légumes pour Madame!*" I looked him steadily in the eyes and replied coldly:

"*Pour MOI, Henri? Ça c'est bien!*"

He looked extremely uncomfortable as he handed his grubby little account for the vegetables sold, and I noticed that although the market was said to be overstocked and the prices obtainable very poor, these were extremely good.

Very clever of Henri. I realised that even if I had had the moral courage to ask him to show me the contents of his *ballot* I should have been told that he was taking my vegetables to market to sell *for me* as I had asked him to do, and I wondered how much money he had made for himself during all the months he had worked for me. Local gossip said that he had already made a small fortune.

I always suspect that his wife, a large hard-featured Niceoise, puts him up to all his little tricks and deceptions, for he is *un bon enfant*, a great good-natured child, naïve enough to confide to a member of my staff, after the episode of the *ballot* and the bicycle, that henceforth he would be more careful and never again *tricher* Madame.

Ah well, in Provence (and perhaps even in England?) all gardeners are said to "make a little on the side," and one must balance *pros* and *cons*. In Henri's case the "*pros*" are: —

1. His perpetual smile (in all weathers).
2. His good heart (a very genuine thing).
3. His patience (inexhaustible).
4. His genuine good humour (a perpetual joy).
5. His *sense* of humour (most refreshing).
6. His glorious strength and health (rare and enviable).
7. His eagerness to help those in trouble (very touching).

All valuable and lovable assets and characteristics.

The "*cons*" are: —

1. His irregular hours (he comes and goes as he wills).
2. His boasting (after all an innocent offence).
3. His generosity in giving my pasturage, my cuttings, and seedlings here and there without my knowledge or consent (no doubt another form of enrichment, but really does me and my garden no harm).
4. The perpetual little cheatings (which, even if checked for awhile, will surely continue).

It will be seen that the *pros* outbalance the *cons* numerically and, in value, weigh down the balances in Henri's favour, and as I am aware that he will 'do' me when and where he can I must increase my vigilance and try to checkmate him. Rather an amusing game at which, with improving health, I become more and more efficient.

For instance, I noticed an unusual eagerness in him to do the household shopping for my forgetful *bonne*. She asked him regularly to buy a ration of horse meat for my little dog. I noticed that the quantity he brought weekly was very small, the quality not very good, and the price extremely high. I suggested to my little friend that in future *she* should buy the meat when she went to Grasse on shopping expeditions for me. This she did and was able to purchase double the quantity of meat of a better quality at half the price, and I now realise that I have surely been paying the butcher's bill of *Monsieur* and

Madame Henri for some months. He only beamed more widely when I told him that his time was so precious for work in my garden that it could not be wasted on tedious shopping for the household.

Until *I* ordered coal and wood from *honest* peasant friends, Henri did this for me and I was told that we needed four tons to fill my coal bins. It did not seem to me that those bins could possibly contain four tons, and so I got in surreptitious expert advice and was informed very positively that they could only hold three. Since when *Madame* orders her own coal, having realised tardily that for many months she has been warming the little house of Henri and his wife as well as her own. When I informed him that I had changed my coal merchant his smile became a trifle rueful — but it did not fade away. We looked into each other's eyes and the corresponding twinkle in both pairs informed their owners that each was aware that in this battle of wits *Madame* had once again been victorious.

But there are things that I cannot possibly track or check. For instance, this year, for the first time since my return to Provence I decided to buy bulbs from Holland and to give myself a really lovely Christmas present. The exciting packages arrived and the Gazelle and I spent a very happy hour sorting them, identifying the names and colours of each variety in that glorious and dangerous catalogue illustrated in colour which had caused me to indulge in such an extravagance; for the price of bulbs, plus the customs duty, is exorbitant.

We planned where each group should be planted, white hyacinths near my little chapel, yellow daffodils and narcissi in the border near the mimosa trees — all carefully thought out with a view to colour effect and suitability of place. On each bag of bulbs we laid a piece of paper with their colour and the place where I wished them to be planted printed in block letters so that Henri could make no mistakes.

He is always nearly as excited as I am (though perhaps for a different reason) when I give him new bulbs or packets of seeds from England or America, unobtainable in France, and when I called him into my Studio to collect the bulbs for planting, his smile has seldom been wider. But, to our horror, he shovelled all our carefully selected bulbs with their labels flying in all directions into his blue apron, and when, in agony that they would all be muddled and mixed after all our meticulous care, we expostulated, he gaily told us not to torment ourselves because HE KNEW.

Well — beside my chapel bloom pink and blue hyacinths, and nowhere have my colour-schemes been carried out.

And it seems to us that the quantity of bulbs ordered and received has been halved. Whose gardens do they beautify at this lovely moment?

Oh! Henri!

We have no proof. We hope we may be wrong, but — we wonder!

Would *you* keep on this beaming, warm-hearted, delightful villain? I think you would, not only because of his beautiful work in the garden, but for the amusement that he would afford you . . .

Some time ago we passed through a really depressing and disastrous period. France appeared to change her

Government daily, and each new one formed seemed to be composed merely by juggling the same ineffectual Ministers into different positions. Prices continued to rise, and strikes to break out:

"*Plus ça change plus c'est la même chose*," I remarked to Henri, a staunch *de Gaulliste*, and asked him what he made of the political situation.

Raising shoulders and hands into a hopeless shrug, he replied in furious tones:

"*Madame, je comprends plus RIEN!*"

For Henri to admit ignorance upon any subject, the political situation must indeed be desperate.

Torrential and unseasonable rains which made spring digging and planting impossible, wild winds which seared and flattened growing plants and vegetables, tore down climbing roses and nullified in half an hour months of the patient toil of gardeners, upset even the fatalistic serenity of my Henri.

In addition to those horticultural miseries, poor Henri had been suffering from toothache, well deserved because for years he refused to visit a dentist. But the pain became so acute, robbing him even of his smile, that at last his wife drove her big coward to the Man of Teeth, who found that nearly every tooth needed attention, and promptly extracted the one that was giving him such pain. Also, I was thankful to see, he removed a black stump in the front row which, because of his perpetual smile, had offended me daily and hourly — with the exception of Sundays and Feast Days — for four and a half years. This was replaced, wonder of wonders, by a new porcelain tooth, and not the gold tusk that I had feared to see, because the Provençaux put their money into golden teeth which remain safely in their mouths till death and then are bequeathed to relatives.

Visits to the dentist became a daily excuse for Henri to leave his work an hour earlier. When he appeared to collect my letters at 4 P.M. instead of 5, before I had time to express surprise he gesticulated despairingly and with his broadest smile cried: "*Le dentiste, Madame!*" and I had to accept his statement. When I remarked sympathetically one day that I feared his dentist bill would be enormous, he reminded me of the equally enormous sums we paid for his physical insurance every quarter.

But how often do we deceive ourselves! Some time afterwards I found Henri, with a brow black as thunder, furiously slashing at brambles which had overgrown a path. Between slashes he told me that the Insurance people had absolutely refused to pay for his dentistry because only two teeth had been lost and replaced. These came under the heading of decoration. It was necessary to lose a minimum of ten teeth before you had the right of compensation, the argument being that without ten you could not eat your food.

"*Toujours des excuses!*" bawled Henri furiously, decapitating brambles as though he wished they were Heads of Government Departments: "*C'est de la tricherie!*" And indeed the Insurance Companies of France do seem reluctant to pay up, however just the claim. I have known cases here — but this book will be entitled 'LAUGHTER IN PROVENCE,' and the instances I could give are worthy of tears, and so I will continue this chapter with another refreshing incident.

One miserably wet evening, before he performed his last duty, which is to bring in a supply of logs and firewood for my Studio fire, I thus addressed THE *derrière*, displayed to best advantage as he neatly stacked my logs in the cavity beneath my raised fireplace:

"Henri," I said in French, "everything is so awful that I believe the end of the world is coming."

Swinging around upon his haunches he faced me, smiling still, and with incredible emphasis spat forth these words:

"*TANT MIEUX!*"

This reply — from Henri — was so deliciously unexpected that my little friend and I stared at him for a moment then burst into uncontrolled laughter, in which Henri, shaking silently, joined, and then we all felt better.

Before this book goes to Edinburgh to be printed I must chronicle the end of Henri's reign here.

A few weeks ago he entered my Studio with a ponderous tread and informed me, with his usual smile, that he had very, *very* bad news to tell *Madame*, who instinctively stiffened her spine to receive it.

He had, he said, decided that he could make more money working for himself, visiting various properties to do expert pruning as he had done in the past for the *horticulteur* in Grasse. But now *he* intended to be master and to pocket all the fees. Therefore he would be leaving

57

Madame in two months time and on Monday next he would be taking his *congé payé* — a fortnight's holiday on full pay . . . This at the season when, in the great heat, vegetables and flowers perish unless they are watered daily; when labour is generally impossible to get because harvests are being gathered in, *jasmin* must be picked and the *vendange* looms ahead of us all and the grapes are nearly ripe.

It was really staggering news, and the fact that Henri was taking his holiday at once instead of after his imminent departure was — rather disgusting. I asked if it would not be possible to defer his holiday, which would anyhow be paid in full, for the climbing roses should now be pruned, the cypress hedges clipped, and a thousand other pressing things done.

He looked very sheepish, but said that his wife was having her holiday from her work in the scent factory and that he was *très fatigué*. Henri! bursting with health and strength, exuding the oil of gladness and prosperity! Henri *fatigué*! In France *fatigué* means ill rather than tired, and I never saw a healthier man than Henri at that moment, though he did look thoroughly ashamed as he made this statement and could not look me in the eyes, for he knew full well that he was behaving badly.

Well — well — well — and perhaps (others who know better than I and do not deplore his departure) believe that it may be well for me in many ways that Henri goes.

Louise says that Henri told her that his wife battled against his decision. From *Madame's Domaine* they had had wine, oil, vegetables, *eau-de-vie*, and many other perquisites which in these expensive and hard days in France cost much money. But Henri was adamant. He would try his luck anyhow, and if he didn't succeed — "*Tant pis*," he could easily find another place as gardener. Always the same buoyant self-assurance.

And so, to-morrow, I see the last of that broad smile and broader stern. I shall miss that oblong patch of contrasting colour on those faded blue trousers, but, I am assured on all sides, I shall cease to miss many other material things.

CHAPTER
FOUR

The Incompleat Bonne

Louise has replaced my beloved Margharita, the faithful *bonne* and friend who shared my life here for so many years and guarded my little home, menaced often, all through the war — Margharita, stolen from me (at the age of forty-five, which I considered safe, but found that there is never safety from marauding men) by a volcanic Italian mason.

I mourned for Margharita, but God was — as usual — good to me, and found me Louise, a pious woman from Normandy with an intense love of men, a notion of cleanliness, and a tremendous sense of humour. Her hyena laugh rings through my little house and refreshes me often, as does the ceaseless clatter of her wooden *sabots* in the kitchen courtyard. She finds the people of the *Midi* lovable, as I do, but their procrastination, their lack of hygiene (to put it mildly), their total lack of time-sense — and of piety — amaze and often exasperate her.

When she arrived here her first question was where she could go to early Mass each Sunday. I gave her the choice of our own village Church perched on the mountain opposite and that of a neighbouring village farther off along the smooth main road. After reflection she chose the latter, judging that in the end this route would be easier and quicker, as she would be saved the steep descent of our small mountain and the still steeper ascent to the little Church opposite.

It was then winter, the weather often variable and the early mornings dark. Undeterred, Louise, tired though she was after all her hard work, for a *bonne-à-tout-faire* really does everything for the household, set her alarm clock at 6A.M., rose, dressed herself, and clumped off to Church in the rain and dim light to attend the Mass to be said at seven o'clock.

Arrived at the Church she found it locked, and waited, fuming in the rain, for the *Curé* to appear. At 7.30A.M. he rolled up — he is very fat and apparently loves his food — and his bed. Louise attacked him at once.

"My Father, I understood that Mass would be said at seven o'clock?" she said gently.

"Yes, certainly, my daughter," he replied a trifle nervously.

"But, my Father, it is now half-past seven," pursued Louise.

The colour of his rubicund face deepened perceptibly until even his ears were tinted as he replied hurriedly:

"I think that clock gains somewhat," as he unlocked the door, positively bustled into Church, and began to toll the bell.

Two peasants sauntered up, and Louise, very cross, for she foresaw that *le petit déjeuner de Madame* would now be served very late, remarked to them that it seemed to her extraordinary that the Mass, fixed by the good *Curé* himself for seven o'clock should be held at seven-thirty. People had their work to do, she said, and now hers would be retarded. She had risen in the dark and walked two *kilomètres* — in the rain — to be in time for the seven o'clock Mass. They chuckled indulgently and congratulated themselves that they lived near the Church and made no movement to get to it until the *Curé* tolled the bell.

Louise, telling me this story afterwards, could not help laughing ruefully as she remarked that in the North they did things very differently, but that she supposed that the southern climate had its effect upon the inhabitants. I could confirm this supposition, for when talking to the Mayor of our village and the *Curé* at our local *Fête* I spoke of the piety of my new housekeeper who, in all weathers, attended early Mass. The Mayor chuckled, and remarked to the *Curé*: "*Pas comme nous dans le Midi, s'il fait mauvais temps on reste au lit!*"

There followed glorious weather, and Louise loved her walk to Church, watching the colours of dawn in the sky and upon the mountains. She was amused and not a little gratified to find that her implied reproach to *Monsieur le Curé* had had an effect, for on the second Sunday Mass was said punctually at seven o'clock.

But she was stupefied on the third Sunday, for the weather had become still more settled and glorious, when the *Curé* announced that he intended to discontinue the early Mass *until the weather became fine* — ! A cynical Frenchwoman, hearing this story, said that when summer came he would probably say that the weather was too hot to celebrate the Mass.

So now Louise descends painfully the steep and rocky track through my olive groves and scrambles breathlessly up the opposite mountain to attend Mass in our own little Church.

There she was struck by the irreverance of the little boys who seemed to be amused at everything, even at the most sacred moment, and she remarked upon their bad behaviour to the civilian in charge. Since when no subdued giggle has been heard and they eye the pious Louise with awe and respect. The smug little girls she described as *sage et mignonne*.

Louise, in a few months, will have reformed and organised us all.

She worked for years with a loved and respected master and mistress, who treated her as their daughter. They taught her the care of antique furniture, its period and history, and they imparted to her their love of the beautiful and the antique, the arrangement of flowers, and the decoration of a dining-table.

When they died she felt lost, and to fill her empty life and heart she went to a derelict *Château* in Normandy, where a Monk had founded a refuge for seventy abandoned children and orphan boys who had been sentenced by tribunals for petty offences and thefts. They have scarcely any funds, but for years Louise selflessly battled on, tending the health of those wild and lonely boys. They learned to call her *Maman Louise*, and she gave them the first love of their lives. Even the hardest and most incorrigible among them would follow her about silently, and they wept when she left.

But Louise was not getting younger, and the indifferent food and hard life began to tell on her health. There was no running water in the *Château* and she took upon herself the duty of washing the sheets and the clothes of the seventy boys — and even the boys themselves. She carried (knowing the heavy weight of linen and especially of wet linen one wonders how) heavy baskets full of sheets and garments down to the river, washed them there, and then carried them back. The water for the daily washing and the weekly baths of the boys had also to be fetched from the river. Hard work even for a man; only firm faith in God and resolve to help suffering humanity could have given her strength to accomplish those tasks.

But friends who had learned to respect and to love her in Provence, whither her late master and mistress came annually to escape the rigours of a Norman winter, pleaded with Louise to leave this arduous work and to think of herself and her precious health for once. I needed a *bonne*, and when they told me what an exceptional woman she was, described as *une perle*, I added my persuasions to theirs with the result that Louise is now here and devoting all the care she lavished on her seventy *gosses* upon ME.

When she arrived she was positively delighted to find me in bed with bronchitis and high fever. That gave her scope to exercise her talent for nursing. Again she was *needed*. She could prepare *tisanes* and *bouillon de légumes*, she could bump up pillows and fuss around me interminably and maddeningly. It was with the greatest difficulty that I prevented her from washing me like a baby, and she was severely disappointed when my doctor did not prescribe injections; for it appears that she is very good at giving *piqures* and longed to stick a needle into me. Her efforts to fatten my emaciated body, now that I am convalescent, are pitiful, for when a dish, prepared with such love and care, sails back untouched or barely tasted to the kitchen in the service lift, she becomes almost tearful. She told me that she daily prays to *le bon Dieu* to give me back complete health and vigour and has given Him six months in which to accomplish this task. He has now only one month to go, but He — and Louise — have really accomplished marvels, and at last I write again after eight months in (and out of) bed when what stands for a brain was like a *purée* of turnips.

I was very grateful to them both when, after so long indoors, I could again go out into my beloved garden and lie in a *chaise longue* in the olive grove. The two terraces below me were purple with gigantic violets, the air scented with their heavenly fragrance. Wild scarlet anemones and blue hyacinths starred the grass around me, and in the distance, perched on its mountain peak, stood Châteauneuf, "the little town of dreams and deep sweet bells," seen through a veil of peach and cherry blossom. Flowers everywhere, above and below me; hyacinths near my little chapel, daffodils and yellow narcissi in the border flanking the mimosa trees; purple crocuses (I think it should be croci — perhaps terminating with two 'i's) in the grass, my Judas tree bursting into bloom above a wall curtained with purple, mauve, and red aubretia, and "*La Follette*," my earliest climbing rose, covering the sun-porch outside my little *salon* and clambering with its incredible growth up and over the mauve-flowered Paulownia tree, garlanding both with lovely blossoms of shaded pink and long-pointed buds.

Louise put me upon my cushioned *chaise longue*, muffled me in scarves and rugs to protect me from any possible chilly breeze, and then brought tea out and set the tray upon a huge slab of stone poised upon a rock to serve as table. Gamine, my odd and temperamental Cocker bitchlet, then sprang upon my lap, thereby making writing or eating extremely difficult, and growled ferociously at anyone who tried to remove her or to approach me.

My expostulations to Gamine were half-hearted; for a possessive Cocker lying upon one's tumpkin is a cosy thing, and acts as an animated hot-water bottle, and so we remained together until the Gazelle came singing towards us to pour out tea for us all.

Louise has become Gamine's "*Nou-Nou*" and slave ever since, when blunderbustering down the few steep steps leading from my Studio to the garden to chase trespassing cats, my little dog strained or displaced a shoulder muscle which crippled her terribly. She made the most of her infirmity and obviously thoroughly enjoyed the gentle massage prescribed by a kind neighbouring vet., to whom Louise carried her like a baby.

She is long since cured and *except* when Louise is around, springs on to my bed with ease. But if Louise is in my room Gamine just rears up on her hind legs, putting two pathetic front paws against the bed and there remains stationary, rolling piteous eyes at Louise as though to tell her she is too weak and ill to spring up, and therefore MUST have her little bot heaved or, better still, be picked up tenderly in her arms and placed in the most comfortable place on the bed. When she tries these tactics upon others, she meets with no success; for we have all seen her leaping from the bed and tearing madly round the garden, over boulders, and down and up steps in chase of — anything — and then watched her tumultuous return and the agile spring back on to her mistress's bed. But this little comedy vastly amuses Louise, who continues to play up to her: "*Madame! regardez donc!*" and then a peal of hyena laughter as she sees what is expected of her by Gamine and performs her duty.

Louise, it will be seen, should have been a Mother, and as she has never married she finds scope for her maternal instinct wherever she goes. I shall never forget her delight when one day I summoned her from the kitchen to help a gallant young mother to bring her latest baby, lying in an English carrying-cot like a glorified washing basket, from her car into my *salon*, nor how Louise purred over that bonny babe chuckling and kicking in its cot while we all had tea, her plain face rendered beautiful by the expression of ineffable tenderness in her eyes.

The two older children ran to her at once, sensing that frustrated maternal instinct in her great heart, and pattered downstairs to the kitchen with her, the little girl demanding a glass of milk *with the skin on it* (UGH!), and the son and heir asking innumerable questions as to the use of this or that; Louise radiantly happy skimming the cream from our boiled milk (alas! all milk, however good, must be boiled here because of the danger of Maltese fever), while the little girl, addressed lovingly as "*Ma cocotte*," perched on her knee and the inquiring boy fingered everything unreproved.

Louise has many friends, but apparently no living relatives, which gives her a hungry interest in everything that concerns us. I am daily asked if I have had any interesting *coups de téléphone*, and if it rings when she is in my room she stands and waits until I have ceased to speak and then eagerly asks me what it was all about. Our correspondence also is of vital interest, and already she has learned to know the handwriting of my brother and sister and the *maman* of my little friend, and joyously brings us those particular letters which she knows we long to receive. Then we are expected to tell her if the news is good or bad.

Her pumping for information has more success with me. I know her to be a lonely but loving woman and that it adds to her happiness to be included in the joys and sorrows of my family. In her case it is merely harmless warm-hearted interest *not* vulgar curiosity. She has less success with the Gazelle, who possesses the Scotch reticence and reserve and also a little devil of mischief, probably inherited from her Irish ancestors, and she loves to tease and to tantalise Louise and resists (*very* gently but firmly) all attempts to be organised.

For Louise tries to organise all our lives starting with that of Henri, who, I discovered one day, had been doing all her shopping. When I found this out I told her his time was far too precious, and that if she did not wish to do the marketing herself there was always my little friend, ready and willing to fly off in the car and do it for her.

Louise replied that she perfectly understood, and that this should never happen again. Blowing dust from furniture with large, pursed lips and removing Gamine's muddy footmarks from the pale-grey tiles of my room with a damp cloth under a vigorously kicking foot (*who* said that it was only possible to do one thing at a time?) she agreed vehemently with me that Henri's time was far too valuable to waste on queueing in shops and market to make petty purchases.

Henri was told the same thing and — *did* I notice a slight tinge of regret in his permanent smile as he realised that in future he must arrive more punctually and no longer have the excellent excuse for coming over an hour late?

Well pleased that that little business was settled, and having provided a block of paper and a new pencil for Louise to note down her requirements as she thought of them and then give the list to the Gazelle, I congratulated myself that this time *I* had done a spot of organising, but — a few days later, when, at the end of his day's work, Henri came up to my Studio to replenish the stock of olive logs for the fireplace and to collect my letters for the post, that dreadful "all-seeing eye" of mine detected a flutter of white apron appearing round the corner of the house where Louise lay in wait for him. Henri must have seen it, too, but he kept a poker face as he bade me farewell, and then my keen ear heard a sibilant whispering and saw Henri's head nod vigorously.

It had all begun again! What is the use of fighting these French? Louise and Henri would certainly go on doing what they want to do and it is less exhausting to close the all-seeing eye and the keen ear and continue to foster *l'entente cordiale*.

So now I allow Louise to organise my gardener and my household affairs.

Very early she found out that the farm that supplied milk to *Madame* was FILTHY, as also were its inhabitants, and that they skimmed the milk illegally and gave short measure. I told her that it was the only farm for miles and that we boiled the milk for a very long time before using it.

Louise, almost tearful, described the miserable condition of the *laitière's* children and hazarded a guess that they were perhaps verminous. I told her that I *knew* they were, for when I inquired after the health of the youngest girl her mother told me that the child was always troubled by her ears, then added an explanatory phrase:

"*Vous savez, Madame, ses vermines portent toujours sur ses oreilles.*" Her vermin — as though we all had them, but *her* vermin always attacked her ears.

UGH —

No sooner had she heard this sinister story than Louise started making inquiries of every peasant she met, saying that unless she could nourish her poor *Madame* with good clean milk she would surely fade away from them all. This started feverish (for them) activity on the part of the peasants around us who, she remarked in a gratified voice, all seemed to love *Madame*. The astoundingly quick result was that in two days a farmer who kept two cows which supplied the milk for *Mademoiselle's* little hospital for the children of St Christophe (now filled with twenty abandoned or orphaned babies) got into touch with a friend who only kept cows for his own family, and persuaded him to supply us. Better still, one of his daughters on her way to her daily work would deliver it to our door. Oh! the relief of that, for hitherto one or other of us had been obliged to trudge for a mile to collect it and sometimes wait an hour for the cows to be brought in and milked. None of us liked that little job, for in wet weather one was invited into an indescribably dirty kitchen-living-room, with an earth floor.

Louise is now triumphant. When the warm creamy milk was first delivered from the new farm she measured it and found that although she had only ordered the same quantity as before, she had gained one full breakfast-cupful, and rushed joyfully to me saying that *la petite* (my poor little friend, who opened wide laughing eyes at me as Louise proceeded) could now go and pay up that dishonest woman.

This seemed to us both decidedly unfair. I was ill and in bed, but why should my guest be drowned in a flood of abuse, as she easily might be? However, she bravely went, paid the bill and delivered my letter, which merely said that I was changing to a farm that would deliver the milk — which this woman had steadily refused to do, although I offered to pay her offspring if they would come — and when she muttered rude remarks, the Gazelle merely professed ignorance of the French language (which she has picked up with wonderful rapidity in less than six months). And that was the end of that.

No, the Italians here in Provence, with exceptions of course, are not clean. Near to the farm live another dirty family, who are my bane. The mother is fat, lazy, good-looking, and smiling; the husband an extremely nice man, who also has his share of good looks. The woman is only twenty-five and gained a Government bonus for producing four children before she was twenty-four. Since then another has been born, and before the year is out there will surely be yet another child on the way, for every year in the early summer the whole family remove themselves to a wooden cabin they have built in the valley below Gourdon amid the orange groves. There they live an *al fresco* life, picking the orange blossom for the *Parfumeries*. The hot sunshine, the intoxicating scent of orange-blossom, moonlight, mountains, invariably have their effect upon that Italian couple, with the inevitable result that I am asked to produce a *layette* the following spring.

An English State-Registered nurse who had taken her C.M.B. was staying in the neighbourhood a year or two ago, and hearing that this woman was near her hour, very kindly walked up to the cottage to see if she could be of any use. She found the doctor already busy, and he asked her to stay and help him with the *accouchement*.

When the baby was born he handed it to her to tend. She searched round the two rooms for olive oil and finding none she whispered: "Doctor, I can't find any olive oil."

He asked her why on earth she should need olive oil, and when she said, "To clean the baby," he opened horrified eyes. OLIVE OIL, precious olive oil to wash a baby! The mother would relapse if she heard that. Olive oil at 1000 francs a litre as it was then — !

He told her to wash the child in the ordinary way, and when she said there was neither running water nor soap in the cottage he suggested talcum powder. There was none of that either. "Then DRESS it!" he commanded impatiently. So having made the baby fairly dry with some of the doctor's cotton-wool and dressings which she filched from his bag, she then dressed the baby in the fourth *layette* provided by me. Contrary to all rules of hygiene the baby prospered.

Louise, as she walks to Church, has already noted those dirty ragged children and will probably insist upon officiating at the next birth, taking with her my softest towels, my most delicate soap, my *Eau de Cologne*, and half the contents of my medicine cupboard.

She boasts about *les belles choses de Madame* as did Margharita, but, unlike her, is extremely generous with my possessions. Everyone who comes to the kitchen must have a bowl of coffee (coffee here is over 1000 francs a pound and bad at that, but I have been indulged in my pet luxury and saved that expense by kind American friends who send me, now and then, lovely coffee berries roasted in the American way to the colour of a cigar). I mourn Louise's generosity with the coffee, but then I remind myself that if I must soon go short, the poor French had *none* all through the war and even now cannot afford it.

Louise has become *une grande dame* in this neighbourhood. Already the peasants sense her superiority of mind and seek her favours. It was a sight to see her *chic* and turbaned, her wild blonde hair caged beneath twisted silk, but still wearing her beloved wooden *sabots*, descend the mountain to visit the owner of the cows who give us this fresh creamy milk, to compliment her upon her virtues and to thank her for helping to strengthen *Madame*. Wine and biscuits were brought forth in her honour and she returned well pleased with herself.

Later I heard that she had informed the neighbourhood, after Mass on Sundays, that she was my *Infirmière* (trained nurse), which fallacy is supported by the white overalls with which I clothe her! Well — if it gives her pleasure and a sense of importance, what matter?

She has a genius for making people work for her. Last Sunday, luckily Henri's day off) all our hens escaped through a hole dug under the *grillage* by some hungry *chien-de-chasse*. In a few moments they were scrabbling among our tender baby lettuces; some had flown up into olive trees, and Louise, half-frantic, had straws in her hair and looked more than ever like a mad March hare; her soft eyes staring and wide, her nose twitching, her large hands gesticulating. She chased them for half an hour, after vainly trying to lure them back into captivity, and then they all took refuge in a thicket of brambles. What was she to do next? Hens were precious. They cost a thousand francs each. They were under her care, &c., &c. Poor Louise!

But at that moment, as she poured forth her lamentations, St Antony, to whom she had been praying to find her lost hens, being perhaps too busy to hunt them home himself, sent a representative to help Louise in the person of Pierre, the chauffeur of an important American who had hired a house on our mountain for the spring and had inundated me with hospitality.

Pierre was bringing yet another invitation, and in a moment Louise had mobilised him to hunt hens — rather hard on the poor young man who was attired in an immaculate white shirt and beautifully creased Parisian trousers. He most nobly ignored his Sunday attire, and in a moment was leaping walls and scrambling up terraces shooing the hens from their hiding places into the open then dashing in headlong chase. He secured all the squawking women, save one, which had sheltered amid a tangle of brambles, and then ran panting and dishevelled to the kitchen. Louise was standing on a wall directing operations and allowing poor Pierre to do the leaping of walls and plunging into thickets.

She told me afterwards, with her hyena laugh, that the young man had actually taken off his trousers in her kitchen in order to remove the burrs and prickly things embedded in them. This consoled her for all.

When I give one of my rare luncheon or dinner-parties, always I engage Francis, a delightful man who can buttle with the best and who takes all the anxiety of service from me. Being bored with bed then, I decided to ask a few friends to come to luncheon, and

Francis came to help us. He arrived looking very smart in his uniform of *Maître d'Hôtel*; he had even been to the barber for a shave and a hair-cut.

This I nosed from afar. I have an uncomfortably keen sense of smell, and into my room on the floor above my little dining-hall, where I could hear Francis busying himself with silver, glass and cutlery, floated a strong and awful smell of exotic scent. It made me feel dizzy and sick, even at that distance, and, in anguish, I called to the Gazelle, whom Louise had deputed to search for appropriate table linen and napkins.

"OH! that scent!" I wailed. "Can it be that Francis has had his hair oiled with some nauseous cheap brilliantine?"

She assured me that indeed he had.

In desperation I rang for Louise, and as I ring my bell only in extreme emergency, she came running upstairs with a white face, thinking, as she told me, that her *petite Madame* was ill. I told her that our dear Francis had become a walking pestilence and smelt to high Heaven — surely *she* must have noticed it, even through the savoury odours that were issuing from her kitchen, if I, on the floor above, was being poisoned? Certainly my guests would be asphyxiated as he served them, and be unable to touch the delicious food his wife (almost a *chef* and hired by us all on great occasions) had prepared for their delectation.

Louise sniffed the air, and then was forced to admit that she *did* notice a slight — something. Francis had doubtless had his hair perfumed by the *coiffeur* in honour of *Madame*'s party, she said, and added tenderly,

"*Le pauvre!*" Now, how to overcome this unbearable situation? If I said nothing my guests might infer that that intolerable stink (an ugly word, but it is fittingly expressive) *came from me*, for English butlers do *not* perfume their hair, and if I asked poor Francis, who had probably paid at least twenty francs of his hard-earned money on a *friction*, to do *something* to diminish its horror I should wound his faithful heart.

I put my problem to Louise, for my guests must soon arrive.

"He must be aired — and at once," she decided firmly, "I will send him out into the garden to fetch logs for the fire and flowers for the finger-bowls, and leaves to decorate the dishes. The hot sun will evaporate the alcohol of the scent, and while he is so occupied I will burn some of the incense that *Madame* keeps for her little chapel."

Wonderful woman! All this she did, and the situation was saved. When Francis returned he left only a faint trail behind him as he moved, and that was soon minified by the incense. No one's feelings were hurt, and my guests could do justice to the fare provided. Only (I hope) to me was the atmosphere of my house slightly reminiscent of a *boîte-de-nuit* and a French Cathedral.

When I gave that luncheon-party it was blossom-time for violets. My two long terraces in the olive grove (violets like semi-shade and here they are usually planted beneath olive trees) were purple with the lovely flowers, as big as small pansies. We picked steadily — for hours it seemed — and I had no less than seven pewter bowls filled with their beauty and fragrance in my little dining-hall and *salon*.

Two days later those terraces were again purple with blossom, and I wondered if I could send some to my sister in Sussex who, like all the English housewives I know, is worn out by the eternal struggle to find food for the family and someone to help prepare or cook it. As she, laughing wryly, poor sweet, puts it: "I've been wedded to the sink for years." In addition, she has the care of a fragile husband. Both he and she share a passion for violets, but they are such delicate and short-lived flowers that I doubted if they would arrive at their destination alive. I asked the Post Office authorities about Air Mail and the manner in which flowers should be sent. They assured me that if the stems were wrapped in wet moss and packed tightly in a carton they would survive the journey by air.

The whole household set to work. Henri went forth to search for moss in the woods; Louise and the Gazelle and I picked violets for over two hours, a back-breaking business in which they did not want me to join as I was barely convalescent after another sharp attack of bronchitis. But I sat upon my gardening "kneeler" between the rows of violet plants so that I could pick on each side. Then I tobogganed on my *derrière* to another patch.

After which came the packing up. I wrapped the stems in the wet moss and helped the Gazelle to place the bunches so close together in their cardboard box that the blossoms could not bruise, and then she did the tiresome part of enveloping the parcel in strong brown paper and stringing it securely while I wrote labels of every description, name, address, Fragile, Perishable, Flowers, Immediate, *Par Avion*, Air Mail, so that all would be fool-proof — I hoped.

I chronicle these perhaps tedious details only to justify the conduct of my little friend, who drove to a Post Office several *kilomètres* away to catch the 4 P.M. mail, which would ensure my flowers' departure from Nice Aerodrome next morning.

The parcel was duly weighed — and the Postmaster whistled and peered at her above his spectacles. She asked the cost by Air Mail, and when he told her that it would be ONE THOUSAND TWO HUNDRED FRANCS she felt dizzy; for she, poor child, must decide whether or not to despatch that parcel and pay that enormous sum, or bring it back to me.

Then the remembrance of the joint efforts of the complete staff of "Sunset House" strengthened her resolution to pay up and send it. Henri, who had spent an hour searching for moss in the woods, returning proud and beaming with a vivid green cushion to refresh the flowers which he had planted and tended for *Madame*. Now they would not only give joy to her family, but spread his fame as a gardener, for surely no other garden could boast of such enormous violets. Louise, her soft eyes glittering with excitement as she picked and prattled of the *émotion* these heavenly flowers would bring: *"Quel couleur! Quel parfum! Quelles énormes fleurs!"* *Madame* tobogganing valiantly along between the rows of plants, so joyous to be once more out of bed and out-of-doors amid her beloved

79

flowers, inspired to fresh effort as she pictured the tired face of that little sister in England — lovelier to her than these violets, but so white and drawn with weariness and anxiety — light into rapture as she opened the parcel, saw such beauty of form and colour and inhaled the liberated fragrance.

No doubt the child also thought of her own aching back, of the boredom of packing that parcel, getting out the car and driving so far to despatch it. Enormous as was the sum, she decided to send it off, believing that I should prefer to pay it rather than disappoint my sister of such joy, and Henri and Louise of theirs in helping to give it. The Postmaster was doubtful; for he considered the price prohibitive and would never pay such a sum for a box of flowers. For a parcel of food, *perhaps* — Being a materialistic Frenchman he could not realise that those violets would provide heavenly food for my sister's soul — far more important than the tumpkin.

My little friend came back and nervously told me of the price and her anxious decision. I told her that if the parcel had cost double the amount *I* should have sent it, and she was comforted. She went downstairs to her room to tidy herself for tea, and heard the voice of Louise in the courtyard below:

"Mademoiselle! Et les violettes? C'était cher d'envoyer ce paquet par avion?"

The child leaned out of the window and told Louise, who was sweeping violently, that awful price.

The sweeping stopped abruptly, and Louise looked up at the window, then quietly remarked with a slight glint of humour in her eyes: "*Ce n'était pas bon marché*," and resumed her sweeping.

It was certainly *not* cheap, and Louise's almost English habit of under-statement made us both laugh immoderately all through tea-time.

God did the rest, for the violets arrived fresh and lovely after only thirty-six hours *en route*, and gave untold joy to the little sister, and her family. And indeed half the village called in to see them, for they lasted for a whole week.

I have hinted that Louise has a love of men. We see evidences of this almost daily, for men of every class and nation continually visit the *Domaine*. When the bell over my great door rings, if she is in hearing she rushes to open it and is sometimes rewarded by finding A MAN standing outside. Then there is a *very* long delay before he is bade to enter and before I receive his message, especially if he is young and good-looking, for Louise engages him in conversation or pays him embarrassing compliments on his appearance. Then I am informed that it is a *Monsieur très chic* who has come to call upon me, or he may only be described as "*très bien*," but always she is pink and giggling, her rather mad, bright eyes dancing with excitement. Certain men she has positively scared with the warmth of her reception, even an attractive young American whom we roped in to help us pick our heavy cherry crop. He asked the Gazelle what was wrong with Louise (I could have told him), and later remarked that she was an extraordinary woman, who seemed to be "suspended between Heaven and Earth" — a really startling description of our Louise coming from the lips of a youth of twenty-seven. But Americans are noted for their powers of observation and a very quick appreciation of the virtues and defects of their fellow men — and women.

During that afternoon of cherry-picking, Louise could hardly be kept away from the tree where that boy was performing wondrous feats of agility. She shouted compliments from beneath, and the Gazelle was sometimes so convulsed by his comments upon Louise that she nearly fell off hers. The boy said, "I've a wicked longing to pelt the old So-and-So with cherries — but she might mistake that for an overture." He muttered remarks about hobgoblins, and said he wouldn't like to meet her alone on Midsummer Eve. All this said in English, of which Louise understands not one word, but punctuated by hyena laughs from her.

Encouraged by his laughter and incomprehensible back-chat she ran indoors to prepare a wonderful iced drink to refresh the young God up in the cherry tree. That afternoon her housework was entirely neglected, but her happiness became complete when at the end of the afternoon the boy courteously visited her kitchen to thank her once more for the delicious iced drink.

Another young man whom she scared to death by her Rabelaisian wit and her too-eager services was the young husband of my niece, both on leave from Kenya after two and a half years' absence. My niece brought her Man to see "her second Mother" (my proud title). He has a magnificent figure, a Greek profile and a shining cap of red-gold hair which covers an excellent brain. And he possesses very blue twinkling eyes — but is very shy.

They had driven across France in a Healey Sports Car capable of terrific speed, and painted in a brilliant shade of green. It is a very small car for passengers, most of the space being taken up by that tremendously powerful engine and a huge reservoir for petrol.

Louise fell for him *and* his car, and her joy knew no bounds when my niece, not knowing that Louise shirks the marketing and always loads it upon the Gazelle, suggested that her husband should drive Louise into the town to do her shopping. The prospect of a drive in such a car (which, wherever it goes, is the cynosure of all eyes and of especial interest to all young men), seated beside *le beau Monsieur*, an object of the envy of both sexes, went to her head like wine, and I was hardly surprised when the poor young man insisted that the Gazelle should go with them as chaperone or he would not go at all! Louise would scream with hyena laughter and make him and his car more conspicuous than they were already; she might do anything —

So they all three packed into that tiny car — Louise told me afterwards that she had hard work to install her well-covered *fesses* and had to roll herself sideways to get in; but she adored her wild drive through the air and the admiring envious glances as they roared on their way. My nephew sandwiched the slim Gazelle between himself and Louise — for safety — and we all realised that the presence of a third had slightly dampened her wild enthusiasm.

I had installed the young couple in what I call "my honeymoon cottage" in the garden so that they might have lazy undisturbed mornings in *"Petit Port"* before descending to my house for their main meals. And I hired a modest village maiden to look after them, prepare their *petit déjeuner* and baths, and so lighten the work of Louise.

But, as I might have expected, it was Louise who went up to the cottage every morning hoping, we were sure, to see *le beau Monsieur*, and the boring work of washing up our dishes in *my* kitchen was left to *la petite*.

During that feverish week of cherry-picking, all hands were commanded by Henri to help. We had already had one thunderstorm, and the rain had caused a large amount of the crop to split and rot. If we did not pick the ripened remainder at once the same thing would surely happen again, for the air was hot and heavy and thunder still growled softly. Anxious about the weather and overwhelmed with work at the same moment, Henri abandoned the garden temporarily for the orchard, and superintended his workers, picking the largest quantity of fruit himself. But for the first time since he entered my service he was irritable and exigeant, and for the first time since she came here Louise found herself bossed by a hard taskmaster. These cherries were for market and, for *his* honour, each must be perfect.

When she showed him proudly her first basketful he pronounced that the cherries she had picked were too red. Louise, allergic to criticism, nevertheless took it from him and thenceforth, mockingly called him *"le Patron,"* but to our amazement did not argue with him.

With us SHE IS ALWAYS RIGHT. There is always an excuse or an explanation for any lapse of hers. For instance, this morning I was obliged to tell her that she had burned the milk and our *café au lait* was therefore undrinkable. I was immediately told, not once but several times during the morning, that the extraordinary taste must be due to the cows having eaten something which caused this *phenomène*. When the poor little milk-woman arrived with the fresh supply, she was made to drink some of Louise's burned milk and was shown an immaculately clean saucepan in which the *phenomène* had been, she affirmed, boiled and NOT burned.

So that we marvelled when she received Henri's adverse criticism in silence.

The poor little Gazelle had toiled all day and caught nothing but blame from *le Patron*. Her cherries were over-ripe and some of them damaged, he said; they would inevitably rot and contaminate others before he could sell them in the market next morning, and he would receive *reproches* and a lower price from the buyers. Poor encouragement for a willing little volunteer!

I think no one was sorry when Henri's weight broke the little step-ladder he was using and he measured his great length on his back in the grass. He was unhurt, but the fall further weakened the stitches securing the patch on the seat of his ragged working trousers. This was unremarked by him but seen by Louise.

He ignored his tumble, climbed a short ladder, and nonchalantly continued stripping cherries (we presume perfect ones) from his tree, leaving his ladder and climbing higher branches to finish his work — "showing off," in fact.

But his dignity suffered a further decline when he tried to descend, for a mischievous broken branch caught in the weakened patch of his trousers. There was a tearing sound, and Louise saw him cast an agonised look over his shoulder — downwards. She knew he wore nothing underneath his trousers in hot weather, so that his disgrace would be complete if the patch tore right away before an audience of two women.

The Gazelle was still shaking with naughty laughter over Henri's tumble off the step-ladder, but being some distance away did not see him in his new predicament, and I am glad to say that Louise had the tact to leave him to extricate himself while she rushed indoors to indulge in peals of hyena laughter in her remote kitchen. Even so, upstairs in bed I heard it — luckily poor Henri did not.

There are too many women on this mountain, and the most tiresome is Minouche, our lady cat. Unlike the rest of us she has many lovers. I cannot call them a goodly assortment; for they are the ugliest set of tom-cats I ever saw, with the strongest lungs and the most persistent characters. At intervals they make night hideous with the terrifying and ear-splitting shrieks and prolonged yowls with which they seek to scare off rivals and to fascinate Minouche. I have tried dead electric light bulbs, which when thrown from a height explode like miniature bombs. In our London garden *Monsieur* and I found these missiles to be intimidating to cats, but in Provence the feline fiends scatter for a few minutes and then return again with exasperating persistence.

One evening I decided to try water. The Provençaux have a strong aversion to washing with water or getting wet with rain. Perhaps a douche of water might prove discouraging to Provençal cats. Accordingly I filled a large jug with cold water and stealthily approached the window overlooking the kitchen courtyard.

I could not see my intended victims because the courtyard is completely covered by a pergola of vines, but I hurled the contents of the jug with irritated force upon this canopy of leaves hoping to swamp the frustrated tom-cats.

There was a wild scuffling and scampering below and a loud human yell. Louise, who had come out to perform the same office, had received the full contents on her head. Then I heard peal upon peal of hyena laughter in the kitchen when she realised that it was *Madame* who had soaked her.

Well — perhaps a chilly douche won't do *her* any harm, bless her.

CHAPTER
FIVE

Gamine

And now I must introduce Gamine.

She was thrust upon me, this tiny black bitchlet.

When I lost my Dominie, the one and only "Blackness," I swore that never again would I put myself in chains — and I really meant it. One suffers too much with them and for them — and, above all, without them — these faithful loving companions who sympathise silently and always understand completely and are so funny — and so wise.

Then one day a friend gave me this warning:

"You say you will never have another dog. Then DON'T go near the Garage Poiret because *Madame* Poiret is keeping a tiny black cocker bitch FOR YOU and insists that you must have her. I've seen her — the last of the litter, very small and entirely adorable. If you see her you'll certainly fall."

So I avoided the Garage Poiret for weeks, making a deliberate detour if business called me to the village where that black danger lay. And then one day, by fatality, I was obliged to pass the garage and just outside it the car suddenly choked — and stopped . . .

In a moment *Madame* Poiret, who lives opposite, had spied me, and in a flash she was across the road — carrying something very small and black. She put it against my neck; it snuffled softly and bit my ear with tiny fish-bone teeth. My heart turned over.

Readers of my books will know — to their cost — that I have Cockeritis very badly.

"*Vous la prendrez?*" asked Madame Poiret with a glint of assurance in her eye. Would I take her?

I nerved myself to pronounce my usual firm refusal.

"No, I will never have another dog," but at that moment the soft and silky person cuddled in my neck, raised her little head and gave me an imploring sidelong look from *human* eyes. I say human because she has that rare thing in dogs, particularly in spaniels, when she rolls her eyes round at you you see the white of the eye, not just the soft iris. This gives an absolutely human expression. She did this, the small black devil, and I was undone.

Without a word I walked to my car, her little black bot cupped in one hand. She gave a triumphant sigh. She had adopted me and I had adopted her. *Madame* Poiret gave an equally triumphant wink.

She must be named, this black baby girl. The Kennel Club of France, where all pure-bred dogs are registered, has a rule that every dog born in a certain year must have a name beginning with the same letter. This was a U year.

What name *could* I select beginning with U?

"Ursule," suggested *Madame* Poiret, but although the little rounded stern and shortly bobbed apology for a tail, docked after the French fashion for Cocker spaniels, did resemble that of a little bear (the meaning of the word Ursula), it seemed to me a most unsuitable name for a dog, and I said so. This problem of nomenclature arose some time after the day of adoption, and already my new possession — or was I hers? — showed signs of a peculiarly devilish though very fascinating disposition. Nothing seemed safe from her depredations, and her *joie-de-vivre* equalled her naughtiness.

"I shall call her The Urchin," I decided.

"*Eeurecheen? Eeurecheen? Qu'est-ce-que-c'est que ça?*" queried *Madame* Poiret, striving to pronounce the name.

Now how could I describe that word in French? At last I said: "*C'est un espèce de gamine.*"

"*Ah! GAMINE! Voilà un joli nom!*" ejaculated *Madame* Poiret, and so my little black devil was named.

She has lived up to that name ever since.

I made a firm resolve — and this time I have faithfully kept it — that Gamine should be everybody's dog, not exclusively mine, and so I allowed friends and staff to feed her, and if I had to go away I left her with some loving person who would tend her as I did. Never again would I be *le bon Dieu* of any dog. In the case of my "Blackness" our inseparability was inevitable, for almost immediately after *Mademoiselle* gave him to me war was declared and my little *Domaine* thrown open to hundreds of French soldiers. They pervaded every corner of the house, the outbuildings and the garden, and my terrified puppy found strange men with loud voices and heavy trampling boots in all his secret refuges and play-places. He was always nervous, and odd noises sent him frantic. Once when I had run down to *Mademoiselle's Château* on some urgent business (she, also, was invaded by the invited Army), I shut the Blackness in my Studio, locking the door so that no one could enter and scare him. Necessity kept me from him for an hour, and when I returned his appearance scared me. His eyes were blood-shot and his muzzle covered with froth. I found foam upon the chairs. They told me that he hadn't ceased screaming all the time I was away. Awful. This must never happen again, the memory of his lonely terror tears my heart still. Thenceforth we were never apart until the war forced me to put him for six months into a quarantine kennel. I never shall know which of us suffered most during that period of time, but I expect I did, for I couldn't explain to my Blackness why we were separated. I visited him every week and spent a long day with him — but, oh! his eyes when I departed — alone.

Though Gamine knew that she belonged to me and was wildly possessive when with me, and extremely unpleasant to anyone who entered my-her-bedroom or my-her-Studio, and absolutely odious to anyone who dared approach me in her presence, she was perfectly consolable in my absence and happy with anyone who made her feel she was in the centre of the stage.

When she grew old enough to scramble up, she took the most comfortable chairs and if anyone tried to displace her, rolled her eyes in a terrifying way, bared her teeth, and cursed that person. I remembered the dogs of a friend in England whom she named Keith and

Prowse for this reason. You remember the slogan of that Firm: "You want the best seats. We have them." Most people were afraid to touch Gamine then, but her fearsome growls meant nothing at all, for she is very gentle, though hopes to be thought fierce. She has had only one lapse. Once she tore the nylons and bruised the calf of a lovely little Duchess who sprang over a low wall into my property where Gamine was on guard. I have often wondered if this was an act of excessive fidelity or if Gamine has been tainted by the smear of Communism in France! I have since insured her against bites — and the tearing of trousers. Very necessary in this country, where certain greedy peasants have been known to ensure a good supply of nether garments without cost to themselves by saying that theirs have been torn by the dogs of the rich. One American woman told me that she had been forced to buy *six* pairs of trousers in one year as some man or other kept complaining that his had been ruined by her dog. Then I told her of the special insurance against bites and trousers, and she rushed off to Cannes to insure at once.

Gamine is by no means a lofty character, but as a puppy she was quite adorable — and adored by everybody, though no one could contradict me when I said that her character was then entirely despicable. She did the meanest things, filching the food of the cat, visiting every bedroom of my house, and trotting up to my cottage in the garden at the hour of *petit déjeuner*. There she would sit, gazing at the occupants with dark, tragic eyes as if to say, "No one has given poor Gamine bite or sup. You lie there enjoying your coffee, toast and marmalade, while I die of hunger." Those awful eyes would roll from one person to another to watch their effect. No one could resist them, so the little black blot on the Fortescue escutcheon devoured sometimes as many as four or five breakfasts until her mistress, noticing with concern the widening waist-line of her voracious puppy, looked into the matter.

After these breakfasts, perhaps to help digestion, Gamine proceeded to torture the hens, rushing round and round their enclosed park screaming with excitement as the flustered ladies within it scurried madly from one corner to another, not realising — for the brain-box of a hen is pitifully small — that they were safely wired in from that black danger. Not good for our egg yield.

Next there were the rabbits to scare out of their wits. One need only rear up on floppy legs, press one's niffling nose against the wire, and emit from time to time sharp piercing barks. The results were wonderful, the poor rabbits running a Marathon race up and down their pens and leaping through connecting apertures.

All this must somehow be stopped.

The little Parisienne temporarily in charge of my kitchen had an uncanny way with birds and animals, who all loved her. She possessed a little mongrel dog with the mouse-like face of a Cairn and the tail of something else, called appropriately *Souris* (Mouse). At intervals Souris strayed from the paths of virtue and produced a most interesting family. One member of these, the queerest mixture of dogs I ever saw, was kept to console her when her other children were given away.

This odd beastlet was called *Mouche* (Fly). A learned doctor, visiting me, happened to see Mouche and exclaimed in utter astonishment: *"Qu'est ce que c'est, ce bête-là?"* What indeed was tiny *Mouche*?

Quick as a flash came the explanation from my little woman: *"C'est un accident des carrefours, Monsieur,"* which reply enchanted the doctor. Little Mouche was indeed an accident at the cross-roads. That remark was a fine example of quick Parisian wit. Souris had just produced yet another family when Gamine entered ours, and I was rather afraid that the jealous little mother might attack my intruder. But, on the contrary, Souris at once adopted the puppy as a member of her family, washed her all over with gentle licks whenever she could get near her, and allowed her to nestle close in the bed-box with her other children.

When Gamine developed her tiresome hunting tendencies, my little Parisienne decided that these habits must be cured. Thenceforth every morning, when feeding-time came, she took my excited puppy *into* the hen-run. The birds fluttered all over her, some sitting on her shoulder as she spooned out their savoury mash, and Gamine got a gentle tap on the nose with the messy wooden spoon whenever she showed morbid interest in any bird. This surprised her, and then her coral tongue, when cleaning up the bespattered nose, found that strange mixture good to eat, so that the morning ceremony became a daily joy. Afterwards she awaited Yvette to visit the hen-run every day, and the poor ladies within it were left in peace during the day. Our egg yield improved.

Then there were the rabbits. These excited Gamine much more for they had a gamey smell. I wondered if Yvette would ever succeed in training her to leave them in peace. And then one morning to my amazement I saw Yvette kneeling on the ground in front of the rabbit hutches holding in her hands a baby rabbit while Gamine licked its little face. Entranced, I watched my puppy "*faire la toilette*" of that baby rabbit. Yvette knelt patiently while the complete ceremony was performed. Every inch of that little furry body was washed by Gamine's pink tongue. Yvette, with her uncanny knowledge of the mentality of birds and beasts, had awakened in my Gamine the maternal instinct.

Rats were seen running around the hen-yard and wood-shed. Henri begged me to get a cat. I cannot like cats, they kill birds, and their character is far too egoistic and aloof ever to attract me. Gamine chased madly any stray cat which ventured into the *Domaine*, and I pointed out that if I procured a cat its life would be pure hell. My gardener, however, persisted. I happened to discuss this feline problem with a neighbour and she said:

"You must have Minouche. She has been brought up *with* my poodle and sleeps in his arms every night so isn't afraid of dogs. If Gamine runs at her she'll roll on her back and tap her nose and think it's just a game — and if she doesn't run away there'll be no fun for Gamine, who only wants the excitement of a chase."

Exactly this happened, and my friend kept one of Minouche's kittens for herself. Minouche and Gamine became great friends, and when the cat produced yet another family Gamine adopted the one kitten we kept to console the prolific Minouche and became its *marraine*. When Minouche left it to take an airing and stretch her legs, Gamine replaced her, getting into her bed and tenderly washing the blind baby kitten as it cuddled up to her.

I shall never forget the first *accouchement* of Minouche in my *Domaine*. For some days we had to dislodge her from dark corners of the linen cupboard and dress cupboard. Then she chose the soft bed in the spare room which was at that moment shuttered and unused. She had firmly resolved to have her family indoors, and completely ignored the lovely bed that I had prepared for her in a warm shed outside.

I was having a big tea-party, which overflowed from my little *salon* into the communicating dining-hall, when my acute ears heard strange sounds. They seemed to come from a tiny alcove under the stairs. *Could* they be caused by rats? I have a horror of them, but never, thank Heaven, had I seen one *inside* my house. Someone had put a raffia shopping basket into that alcove, and suddenly I heard a piteous "miaow," saw it tilt over upon its side, and then realised that Minouche's hour had come and she was in the act of giving birth — in the shopping basket.

At intervals, while prattling to guests, I heard a sharp "miaow," but no one else noticed it. When my guests had all gone I told my niece that I was certain that Minouche was having her family in that basket. I am entirely ignorant of the *accouchements* of cats — and so was she. We fetched a big Veterinary Dictionary, hoping to learn from it what we ought to do. We searched under every heading — Gestation, Pregnancy, &c. — but the author of that volume seemed only to be interested in pigs, cows, and horses.

"Ought I to go and hold her paw to comfort her?" I asked.

"Ought she to be fed with brandy or milk between kittens?" Above all we wondered if she should be transferred from the narrow shopping basket to her warm bed.

I agonise over trifles, and the *accouchement* of Minouche was an anxious event. My niece, also a lover of animals and as inexperienced as I, was equally upset. It was pouring with torrential rain outside, but she gallantly volunteered to rush up our mountain to the abode of a very charming man, a retired vet. who, nevertheless, continues to care for the health of the animals of our peasant neighbours just for love. He would certainly advise us. The eager child sploshed forth into the deluge and was gone for some time. On her return she told me that the great barred gate of the vet.'s house was padlocked, but, undeterred, she clambered up and over it. He was lost in admiration of this feat of agility, "*mais les Anglais sont très sportifs,*" and had been gently amused by our anxiety about Minouche. We were to leave her absolutely alone — cats managed their affairs extraordinarily well. Just put a saucer of milk near the basket and — go to bed. The family should normally appear at intervals all through the night. Should Minouche seem uncomfortable in the morning he would come at once and help her.

Gamine was morbidly interested in that quivering shopping basket which moved in an uncanny way at intervals, and we had to shut her up in my room. When we placed the prescribed saucer of milk in the alcove last thing at night we heard to our delight a soft rhythmic purring. All must be well, for Minouche was singing a lullaby to her babies.

It was one of these that Gamine adopted. Obviously she must one day be allowed to have a family of her own. But where to find a suitable and beautiful husband? Her local admirers are all "mongrels, puppies, whelps and hounds and curs of low degree," and the most favoured, who pays her nightly visits, is a cross between a St Bernard and an Airedale, with the colouring of a wire-haired terrier. He is very far from beautiful, but amiable, charming and adored by Gamine, who when he bends down to kiss her puts her arms around his neck whining with loving welcome while her little black stern waggles with delight and her whole body squirms with ecstasy. Oh! why do women so often fall in love with unsuitable men?

Perhaps one day I may be driven to — well, I will tell you a story of a little adventure that happened to Gamine and me. We were walking down the main road which passes through our village of Opio; Gamine, on the lead, looking very beautiful and towing me along at a frantic and uncomfortable pace in order to get swiftly to olive groves when she can run free without danger from passing cars. From the direction of Cannes came a small Fiat. In it were two fat, smiling people, a man and a woman, quite obviously *bourgeois* French, with a black Cocker spaniel sitting between them.

They espied Gamine and their smiles grew wider. Two more victims of Cockeritis, thought I, and my heart warmed towards them. They stopped the car and swiftly opened its door. In a trice their spaniel was across the road and nose-to-tail with Gamine, while its owners peered out anxiously.

"C'est un male?" they queried excitedly, and when I told them that Gamine was a female they threw up their hands with a gesture of bitter disappointment and ejaculated: *"Malheur! le notre est aussi une femelle — et c'est le moment."*

What a wonderful way of evading the payment of a stud fee, to tour the countryside with a lady in an interesting condition and if, by luck, you should meet a suitable husband for her — well! just stop the car — and open the door.

How French! How delightful!

Equally French is my last little story of Gamine. It was Louise's day off and unluckily for her a thunderstorm had broken and rain poured down.

She had begged to be allowed to take Gamine with her to visit some old friends in a neighbouring village. Their little girl adored *la petite bête* and loved to take her for walks and to pretend that the beautiful Gamine was her own. I was driving along the main road from Grasse to Nice when suddenly I espied Louise walking homewards towing a most extraordinary white object. She was wrapped in a long cloak, and was unmistakable because of the peculiar rolling gait caused by wearing

Norman *sabots*. Behind her, open, and apparently lying on the ground, was the enormous blue Provençal peasant umbrella I had lent her as a protection against a possible storm.

Thoroughly puzzled, I accelerated and drew up alongside.

The white object was my poor little black Gamine, enveloped in newspapers and tied up with string like a parcel to protect her from the rain — *a spaniel*! The open umbrella behind them sheltered the little girl — she was squatting under it in a ditch, relieving nature. The rain must have given her ideas.

Could — and do such things happen in England?

CHAPTER
SIX

Fun in Fever

Yes! one *can* have fun in fever — if it's high enough to give one delusions and to make the real unreal and the unreal real; a delightful mixing up of past and present, when material things cease to matter and one enjoys adventures with Beloveds long since translated to a happier sphere. No longer is one gonged into meals; a sip of barley-water is enough or orange juice administered occasionally. The visits of a doctor, complete with black bag and stethoscope, daily ablutions and the changing of bed-linen are the only necessary things which disturb the peace prescribed for the feverish. After these one is left to dream between cool sheets. For a time no fussing, no formalities, no housekeeping, no effort of any sort either mental or physical. Other people take up one's burden of life. It is really rather delicious.

I have only nice delusions, and am always surrounded by the Beloveds who come in and out. But in Provence my fevers are enlivened and my peace disturbed by my peasant neighbours. They are told that *Madame* is ill and must not be disturbed, but they are fond of her and naturally wish to find out for themselves *how* ill she is, and so they slide in through the door of the Studio and from thence into my bedroom, thus avoiding the vigilance of Louise working in the kitchen below.

They start conversation in low tones, asking in anxious whispers: "*Comment ça va, Madame?*" and when I say with a smile: "*Je suis toujours en vie,*" they laugh and take heart. In a few moments they are pouring forth their own troubles, and their little joys.

The other day we had a *bal masqué* in the village, and the excitement of the neighbourhood was intense. Every man wished to disguise himself as a woman and every woman as a man. My bedroom was invaded by would-be masqueraders asking the advice of *Madame* and what clothes could she supply to make a Chinaman — or Chinawoman, an Indian, a Hottentot, a Spanish matador, and so on. I do not keep a theatrical wardrobe, so my fevered head was obliged to think out possibilities from my own clothes cupboard. I did manage to equip my once temporary cook with a Chinese coat and a pair of trousers, which must be banded at the ankles, but when I heard, later, that she had capped this Chinese costume with a wide felt sombrero turned up on one side and decorated with the handsome tail of a cock killed for home consumption at the feast of *Mi-Carème*, I felt that I needn't really worry much about the correct details of costume.

Everyone wanted to look *saillant* or *rigolo*. My cook must certainly have succeeded in looking striking, and my washerwoman, with a mask decorated with a red nose and wearing her husband's clothes must have looked very funny as her cavalier. Eight couples were to enter two by two in procession, preceded by a gentleman playing the accordion.

Apparently the evening was marred by the ignorance of *étiquette* shown by several rowdy boys, who tore off the masks of the ladies in the procession thereby revealing their identity *before midnight*. This caused general indignation, and a resolve in future to boycott the *café* of our village and to resort to another a few miles away, where people knew how to behave.

One poor little woman, who was to have been in the famous procession, mourned that an ancient aunt of her husband had inconveniently died that week and thus prevented her niece-by-marriage from joining in the festivities. It did seem hard that *un petit deuil* should be necessary at that particular time. The mother-in-law of another reveller had the tact to die *after* the *bal masqué* and spoiled nobody's fun.

My fevered sleep during that time was enlivened by visions of Chinese ladies with plumed hats, red noses, and crêpe weepers. Great fun.

Big Henri was the most persistent invader of my bedroom. When he came to bring wood for the Studio fire and to collect letters he would always ask for a little word with *Madamè* — some question about the garden. From my bedroom I urged him to speak, but this was always the signal for him to burst through the curtained doorway and to stand, a beaming Hercules, at the foot of my bed. This enabled him to report to the inquiring neighbourhood whether or no they should order their wreaths for my interment. His rubicund visage and unruly curls and his boundless vitality probably did me more good than many medicaments, and always he made me laugh.

It was suggested that I should go to Luchon, in the *Pyrénées*, for a cure. The natural sulphurous springs gouting forth from subterranean sources there are radio-active, and work wonders for people with afflicted bronchial tubes and for those crippled with rheumatism.

Luchon is a lovely little town in a valley between high pine-clad and often snow-capped mountains. It is washed by excitable little torrents which rush down the gutters on either side of the streets, clean, fresh and invigorating, providing cheap foot-baths for the aged poor, and sport for the very young, who launch paper boats which rush madly downstream to the accompaniment of excited yells from the master mariners. In the summer season males, old and young, play a game with a captive ball attached to a long rubber string. They play on pavements and capture unwitting pedestrians; they play in the streets to the rage and frustration of motorists, and half the town makes suggestions when the ball flies up into a tree and is caught by the branches.

In the autumn the youth of Luchon roller-skate amid the traffic, and in the evening, when it dies down, races are organised down the main boulevard, parents encouraging their young from upper windows or accompanying them on bicycles, shouting warnings and instructions. The Luchon police merely look on at this extremely dangerous sport, but I never saw a *bâton* raised in rebuke. People taking the cure sit outside the numerous *cafés* under gaily-coloured umbrellas, enjoying an *apéritif* or a coffee between treatments at *Les*

Thermes — a great, white-columned building set in a lovely verdant park near a non-sulphurous ornamental lake.

I went there first, one September, with a hardworked brother. He enjoyed his mountain expeditions as much as he loathed the sulphur-water gargles amid noisy Frenchmen, who seemed to vie with each other over who could gargle, spit, and snort with most effect. And except for the treatments at *Les Thermes* he loved the life of the little French town, and was always escaping to some *café* or other for a cup of coffee and a *palmier* (a sticky pastry affair shaped like a palm leaf), or to sip an *apéritif* with some strange French name as he watched the animated life of Luchon flow past him.

In June of the following year I returned alone, caught a chill during the complicated cross-country journey, and was obliged to spend my first twelve days in bed with a temperature varying between 103 and 104. But I had been given a ground-floor bedroom overlooking the main *boulevard*, and I never had a dull moment. From my bed I had a marvellous view of all subsequent events, and it was like watching an exciting cinema show in the greatest comfort. I was never lonely, though apparently stranded alone and ill far from home in an hotel. All my Beloveds came to me in turn and laughed with me and enjoyed the varied scene.

It was the season of *Pentecôte*, and down the great *boulevard* edged with blossoming lime-trees — which scented my room deliciously — fluttered little white brides, like flocks of doves, their tulle veils billowing in the breeze; the little girls of Luchon going to their

105

Première Communion. They seem so pitifully young to take solemn vows, but He did say, "Suffer the little children to come unto Me." Their tiny sins confessed the night before to the old priest — a fib told to *Maman*? A *bon-bon* filched from the family box? Disobedience? Laziness? Perhaps impertinence? Their faces now are calm, radiant and reverent, little masks of purity. For the moment they are God's angels. May He grant them a right judgment in all things and make them rejoice in His holy comfort as they grow into women, with all the cares of life — and perhaps motherhood before them. So I pray from my bed.

White snow scintillates in the bright sunlight upon the highest mountain peak; white oxen, lumbering slowly down through the forest and lugging timber from the mountains, cross the procession of little white brides, bells tolling from their carved yokes; flocks of clean white sheep with skipping hungry lambs striving to gain nourishment from ewes that seek only to avoid the terrifying traffic, the yapping solicitude of the sheep-dogs, and to gain swiftly the haven where they would be.

Some way behind this procession of white beasts and little white brides a very small brown girl, perhaps seven years old, prances astride a baby black donkey; she represents joyous original sin and seems to glory in it. Her aim seems to be to distract the serious attention of the little brides by suddenly digging her bare heels into the flanks of her steed and galloping through their lines, causing them to flutter aside like frightened doves. Her naughty laughing face is somehow a refreshment to a sinner like me, and I love her mischievous pranks and the sense of life and liberty she brings. She is one of God's *gamines*.

Every evening during the Feast of Whitsuntide there was always something picturesque and exciting to watch. I would be wandering in our old *Domaine* with *Monsieur*, admiring the success of our joint efforts to beautify it by planting flowers with much hope and faith but with little horticultural knowledge; showing Mummie, who had somehow drifted into the garden, bringing with her, as always, light, loveliness and laughter, the tiniest rose-bush in the world (it took the great Clarence Elliot five years to perfect so that each miniature blossom became a real double rose — the wee bush was so small that it must be pruned with nail-scissors), when suddenly we heard a galloping of hooves and the blare of silver hunting-horns, and we were all back in Luchon watching the Mountain Guides, clad in black and scarlet, riding by on their prancing horses, cracking their whips in unison like pistol-shots in the cool scented evening air. Behind them danced the Luchonnais maidens, chosen for their beauty and grace, wearing the picturesque festal dress of the women of the *Pyrénées*, full black skirts, scarlet bodices ruffled with white cambric and lace. Their cavaliers were singing their wonderful song, "*Les montagnards sont là*," which I had heard homesick soldiers from the *Pyrénées* sing in our little *foyer*-tent at Opio, in 1939, as they danced *le Bourrée* around the trestle-tables with the rain pouring down and trickling through the tent, turning the ground beneath their dancing feet into a morass of mud.

107

And there was *Mademoiselle*, my beloved Elisabeth Starr, sloshing around in gum-boots, her great dark eyes laughing as she placed empty beer-bottles on the tables under the worst of the leaks to catch the trickles of rain-water.

"Nothing matters, Pegs, they're happy for a moment" — and then we filled endless cups with hot chocolate from a gigantic urn and were surrounded by a waving mass of eager outstretched hands . . .

A knock on my door, a sudden blaze of electric light which scared away my Beloveds, and there stood my devoted doctor ready to sound my wheezing tubes and take the hurrying pulse. He was full of concern for what he considered my lonely plight and my noisy bedroom; astonished to find me smiling and serene, thoroughly enjoying myself.

After the doctor appeared the old *femme-de-chambre* with the amazing and appropriate name of Généreuse. She adopted me as her own and brought me cups of *bouillon de légumes*, that wonderful juice of all the vegetables in season, sovereign remedy of the French for most ailments, especially a feverish condition.

I fell asleep lulled by the strains of blaring radio sets in neighbouring *cafés*, the yells of excited children, and the distant strains of the town band playing on the big open square outside *Les Thermes*. It was all delirious and fantastic and amusing, whether sleeping or waking.

Another night Luchon was visited by the band of the Guides of a neighbouring mountain village. This was perhaps the most picturesque procession of all. Men attired in baggy white breeches striped at the sides and banded at the ankles with vivid emerald green. They wore loose tunics of emerald green and *bérets* to match, and from their silver hunting-horns fluttered *fanions* of emerald green. The youth of Luchon, desiring a better view than that provided by the electric street-lamps half-hidden by bosses of lime blossom, lit Roman candles in the gutters so that the whole street was illumined by an almost unearthly light. It shone upon the handsome brown faces of the Guides, on dark shining eyes full of life and laughter, on gleaming white teeth. They swaggered by, twirling their silver hunting-horns, the little green flags waving and twisting when they raised horns to their lips and provided melody for the accompanying drums.

"Madame s'est bien amusée?" Généreuse with her soothing soup. And so to sleep, perchance — nay certainly — to dream.

Convalescence at last! Now I could start "the cure" in good earnest. On payment of the necessary sum I was given my card of entry to *Les Thermes*, where, in the various spacious rooms, different treatments are given of varying strength. I was astounded by the long memories of the attendants, who all remembered me from the year before; one and all desired news of my brother and asked me why he had not come to take the cure with me.

In the room where *Humages* are given, one is seated before a mouthpiece from which issues the sulphurous steam from the subterranean springs, which one gently inhales for the prescribed time. There are several controlled springs, some stronger than others — little children are given *Source Blanche*, the least pungent of all.

Dozens of people of all sexes and denominations and ranks, from tonsured monks to pretty little *cocottes*, rich Americans, and ragged French peasants sit in long rows in various moods of boredom or intense concentration. Some prop books or newspapers behind the mouthpiece and while away the time of inhalation by reading. Pathetic peasants glare into the mouthpiece and breathe noisily to inhale their true money's-worth of curative fumes.

Mouth and nose pressed into the receiver, my eyes could still wander and roll from left to right enjoying the study of my fellow creatures. The children delighted me most. Immediately a child of Luchon starts a cold or sore throat he — or she — is bundled off to *Les Thermes* for an inhalation upstairs, or downstairs for a gargle. They are so accustomed to this procedure that the treatments no longer scare them, and mothers leave mere babies, two or three years old, in charge of elder sisters of perhaps six or seven. *Maman* points to the great clock at the end of the long hall and tells the child in charge exactly where the minute-hand of the clock must point when the treatment is over. She places her baby upon a high stool, presses its button nose and often protesting mouth into the receiver, and then leaves the youthful guardian in charge with a last admonitory pointing of the finger towards the great clock.

Then the fun begins. The baby is at first still under the restraining influence of *Maman*, but this soon wears off. The little head lifts and turns to have a peep at other inhalants. The small sister seizes the baby's head and twists it round again, and with a peremptory *"Allez-y!"* the button nose is forcibly pushed back into the receiver; but the eyes still wander. If I am sitting next door our rolling eyes meet in sympathy as we breathe in that noxious odour of bad eggs. Gradually the little head also turns in my direction, but instantly its guardian twists it back again and repeats irritably *"Allez-y! Mais — Voyons!"*

It is a little difficult for a child to sit still for perhaps twenty minutes, while other luckier ones run wild races up and down the long hall between the double row of chairs, awaiting the moment when *Maman* or *Papa* or *Grand-Père*, undergoing treatment, will rise with a gusty sigh of relief, mop their faces, damp with sulphurous steam, wind mufflers around their mouths and throats, collect their offspring and depart. Try to imagine the out-patients' department of an English hospital or dispensary with a crowd of small children dragging little model trains or motors, playing ball and catch-who-can up and down the wards and passages while their parents undergo treatment! But in France *la famille* is everything, and children accompany their parents everywhere. Certainly their noisy antics enliven a boring treatment, but they would not be permitted in the quiet orderly life of our perfect English medical services.

As I grew stronger my various treatments were increased to eight a day, and I spent my time between *Les Thermes* and the hotel chosen for me by my doctor because it was almost opposite. On Sundays the great Thermal establishment is only open until noon, and I

111

was obliged to rush around the building trying to fit in as many treatments as possible before the electric buzzbell buzzed us all out into the open and the great doors clanged together with, it almost seemed to me, a big bang of relief.

On Whitsunday the *Fête-Dieu* was to be celebrated, and also the election and crowning of "*Mademoiselle Luchon*," the prettiest and most charming maiden of the town, who was to be borne in triumph through the streets in a flowerdecked and canopied litter by the handsomest youths that could be found.

I longed to see and to applaud *Mademoiselle* Luchon, for I love youth and beauty, but I feared that my boring treatments in *Les Thermes* would cause me to miss all the fun.

Sunday in France ends at noon, and thereafter the day becomes a secular feast. If I rushed across the square to my hotel when the buzzer buzzed I might yet be in time to watch *Mademoiselle* Luchon carried past in her litter. Just before I reached the hotel I saw a golden canopy sailing along the pavement amid a crowd of people, followed by a pip-squeak drum and fife band. The crowd of Luchonnais was so dense that I could only see the moving golden canopy but not the figure that it sheltered.

Addressing a group of French people on the steps of the hotel I exclaimed excitedly:

"*Mademoiselle Luchon! C'est Mademoiselle Luchon?*"

Countless pairs of eyes turned upon me with a stare of shocked horror.

It was the Archbishop carrying the Host ... The ceremonies of *Le Fête-Dieu* were just ending ...

That I, with my deep respect for French Catholics and my reverence for all their religious observances, could make such a terrible, such an unforgivable *gaffe* ...

I crawled up the steps of the hotel practically on all fours, and hid my shamed head in my bedroom, wondering how I should ever dare to show my disgraced face in public again.

I had watched, with *Monsieur*, the wonderful ceremony of *Le Fête-Dieu* in Grasse years before, when every house was decorated with lovely hand-embroidered quilts, centuries old, hanging from balconies of hand-wrought iron, one of the great industries of Grasse; had told my little Protestant beads before flower-decked altars at street corners and the embrasures of shop entrances. Together we had admired the wonderfully decorative effect of the very poor, who, for the honour of God, had hung cotton sheets sewn with the heads of real flowers behind the altars. We had then watched the lovely faces of little children as they gazed in awe at the great altars and scattered flowers upon their steps.

The streets had been cleared by the police for this procession, and when the great moment came, the Archbishop, preceded by a chanting choir of priests and followed by all the children of Grasse and, indeed the whole population, had walked slowly down the centre of the street under his gorgeous canopy carrying the sacred Host, while the inhabitants of the houses he passed rained down blossoms of golden broom which fluttered in the sunlight like thousands of yellow butterflies and formed a glorious carpet of flowers for his feet.

Let this be my excuse for apparently inexcusable behaviour. In Luchon the Archbishop walking the pavement while traffic and tourists continued to roar down the main avenue — that pip-squeak band — !

But it was still done for the glory of God — and most surely He has a sense of humour or He could never have created ridiculous puppies — and curious people like me.

At least I am sure that *He* pardoned that truly awful *gaffe* of mine — that awful, AWFUL *gaffe*! Perhaps He even twinkled.

CHAPTER
SEVEN

'Ullo! 'Ullo!

I will begin by saying that I hate and fear the telephone, yet I must immediately admit that without it I am lost, and when my line is out of order — which is often — I realise what a vital necessity of modern life it is, especially if one lives on an isolated mountain far outside a town.

All the same I am certain that much misery and many misunderstandings between friends are caused by this useful though dangerous machine.

To start with, it completely alters the tone of almost every voice, often rendering them unrecognisable. This *can* be amusing. I remember once answering our London telephone one evening in my youth. I unhooked the receiver and a delightfully deep and impassioned voice, unknown to me, addressed me thus:

"My Darling! Oh, my own dearest, *when* can I see you? I don't know how I can exist till I see you again, you are so sweet and so very, very lovely."

I was so taken aback that I did not interrupt this glorious flow of language at once — and — he *did* sound rather a poppet (as my nieces used to describe an attractive man). But I *did* abstain from "taking him on," and my silence must have warned him that all was not well, for he then said, nervously:

"Is something wrong? You *are* Miss X.?"

"You make me almost wish I *were*," I replied laughingly, "but I fear the Exchange has given you the wrong number."

"I am much intrigued," he said. "You have such a delicious voice and obviously a sense of humour. *Couldn't* we meet? May I know your name?"

"Great persons often prefer to remain incognito," I answered, "and if you can hardly exist until you see your lovely lady why not scold the Exchange and try for her number again?" Then to mitigate my gentle rebuff, I added, "You, also, have a delightful voice. Goodnight, fair Sir," and I rang off.

That was an amusing telephonic accident, but it is between friends that the infernal machine can make estrangements, for one cannot choose a moment for a conversation which is convenient to them. You may interrupt a quarrel or, worse, a love-scene, perhaps a domestic crisis when it is impossible for the friend to explain the situation, the people involved being in the same room. Your call may collide with — or delay — an important call being anxiously awaited. The receiver may be hung up abruptly, and you are left chilled and unhappy, perhaps even offended until you hear the explanation. During a telephone talk one cannot see the twinkle in an eye, the whimsical twist of a mouth or the elevation of an ironic eyebrow, and so something said in jest may hurt or often offend a hyper-sensitive person.

For these reasons I hate and fear the telephone, nevertheless when I first came to little Opio I never ceased to badger the Telephone Authorities until I got one installed, having learned its full value when my precious Man fell ill in our first *Domaine* and it was vital to get the personal help or counsel of a doctor at any moment of day or night.

A long battle I had; for *Mademoiselle* of the *Château*, the most important householder on our mountain, had steadily refused to have her peace disturbed by such an apparatus, or her property disfigured by posts and wires, and our other dear neighbour shared her dislike of it. So that the Postal Authorities objected that the expense of bringing the line from the main road just for one lone widow was not justified.

However, they did it eventually, whereupon *all* my neighbours found it so convenient to have a telephone near at hand that they one and all used mine, and the Authorities soon found that it had been worth while after all — and *I* began to wonder!

We *have* a public telephone in the tiny Post Office of our village, but the Post Mistress has a large family to keep, and to supplement the income paid to her by the P.T.T. she and all her family work for the scent factories of Grasse; first picking *les roses de Mai* and later helping with the *jasmin* harvest, which may go on till early autumn. And the Post Office is locked up while the family is absent. One of her sons took charge at one moment, but enlivened the boredom of waiting for people to come in to telephone or buy stamps by playing his accordion, which drowned all knocks at the locked door, however insistent. Someone knowing the ways of the house walked round to the back, traversed the kitchen, and entered the room reserved for postal activities. There she found Jacques lying back in a chair, a cigarette dangling from his mouth, his feet on the counter, playing his beloved accordion, of which he is no mean performer.

The village Post Office — WHEN open — closes at noon until, at the earliest, 2 P.M. while the family enjoy their hard-earned *déjeuner*. But it is liable to remain shut much later than that if the daily incoming post (which arrives by bus at 7.30A.M.) has not yet been delivered; for if no member of her family is on leave and she can find no other friend to deliver the letters, the little Post-woman must make the long and mountainous *tournée* herself, and then the Post Office is locked up and is untenanted till her return, which may not be until 3.30 or 4 P.M. The official closing-time is 6 P.M., and on Sundays our Post Office is hermetically sealed all day. So it will be seen that to telephone from our public call office is always difficult and sometimes impossible, which explains the popularity of mine. *I* am thankful to possess the service of Grasse, open all day and night.

For some time we have had an influx of American tenants in the houses on our mountain. American efficiency and "hustle" in all public services are well known. They like their mail punctually and their telephone messages put through swiftly, and they often find our village habits exasperating. I tell them that in Provence they need endless patience, two strong hands, one to push and the other to stroke, but, above all, a

118

sense of humour. I love my Provençaux, and after all these years spent among them I understand them pretty well. But even I become exasperated at times, and I was really angry the other day — I think with just cause.

I had been awaiting two or three important letters, one containing a cheque which I had asked to be sent by Air Mail. Several mornings passed away and no letters were brought to me. The weather was wet and thundery and all our nerves were on edge. We were also missing Henri badly, for he was taking his *congé payé*, in bits, and was absent for over a week. We realise how much we depend upon Henri when we no longer have the comfort of fresh bread brought with the French newspaper every morning from Grasse and must go forth in the car to post important letters.

Great was our relief when his holiday came to an end and he returned to work beaming more broadly than ever. But when he reached my Studio door his smile had become a little rueful; for he held in his hands a bundle of rain-sodden letters — those I had been so anxiously awaiting. Some of the envelopes had perished and the addresses were practically indecipherable. He had found them lying in the scrub near his toolshed at the top of the garden near the little gate, locked in his absence, having been thrown over the fence by our Post Mistress to save herself the descent from the garage down to the service entrance to the *Domaine*. Finding Henri's gate padlocked she had concluded that he was late for his work and would find the letters and deliver them to me later on. Apparently she had lately made a habit of this — everyone seems to make use of Henri — to save her poor weary little legs a few extra yards of stony road. It was unfortunate for her that he happened to be on holiday, so that my letters had remained lying unseen in the wet grass and sodden by torrential rains. Even the weather was against her.

I am very fond of that little woman, one of our oldest peasant friends, and because I know all the difficulties of her private life I have hitherto refrained from complaints that my letters are delivered irregularly and nearly always late (except when we have brisk and exacting Americans living on our mountain), but this time I felt obliged to report the fate of my letters to the *Receveur des Postes* in Grasse, and I enclosed the sodden envelopes as proof that I had just grievance. I also added a personal letter telling him of my respect and affection for our little Post Mistress and begged him not to scold her too much, for I knew all about her hard life and her gallant efforts to do the work of home and Post Office. I suggested just a *very* gentle poke from his august finger.

Apparently he did poke — and poke hard, for I received a most pathetic letter from the culprit, deeply wounded that so old and valued a friend should have reported her to Headquarters, and did I know that her husband was drinking again *and* running after other women; that one of her sons was ill in a sanatorium, another had had an accident on his motor bicycle and was in hospital, and one of her girls was about to have a baby. All quite irrelevent in an official sense, but of course I felt the worst kind of brute.

However, her heart-wound was healed by a *litre* bottle of oil, some wine and a food parcel for the Christmas family feast, and my letters have since been delivered (still at all hours, but one can't have everything) to Louise at the kitchen door.

Newcomers to this neighbourhood are finding it less difficult to get a telephone installed. At one time it took at least a year, because of a lack of material and labour, so that a friend and neighbour of mine was positively electrified when, after a delay of only six weeks, she was informed that the van of the P.T.T. was parked in her drive and men had already been at work for an hour before she woke.

Their arrival coincided with a note from her to me written overnight asking permission for her line to traverse a section of my property. The Gazelle leaped down the mountain with a reply from me saying that it was quite unnecessary to enter my property at all, since there was a telephone pole on the limit-line which could cross five metres of *her* land, which had been especially reserved for the purpose of visiting a *bassin* of water. The Gazelle returned with the information that the *Postes et Téléphones* van was drawn up in the courtyard of the house and the men already hard at work putting the necessary post in the wrong place.

I was naturally indignant that my permission should be asked for this line to cross my property when the deed was already done, and I demanded that the Chief Engineer should come up at once to see me. Equally disconcerted by the unheralded arrival of the P.T.T. my neighbour sent him up at once, and I recognised in him an old friend, a lean dark man with a jutting jaw on which grew a week's growth of black beard. With dancing blue eyes and a very honied and persuasive tongue he at once assured me that I should not even see the telephone wire crossing my property, and that if, when it was placed, for some reason or another I should wish to have it removed, the P.T.T. would AT ONCE remove it. If I wished to confirm the truth of this I had only to telephone to the Head Office in his presence. We smiled amiably at each other, and I lifted an expressive eyebrow and remarked that *should* I give permission and then regret it and make such a request to the P.T.T. it would be granted only when I had been removed to another sphere. He laughed and waved dissent. We bandied words for some time, but I remained firm, pointing out that the line need not traverse my property.

Then out came the truth. The work was nearly done, the post already put up, there was now only the wire to place. If I insisted that it should not cross my land they would have to dig another hole and place the post farther on. Also another post would be necessary and this would cause more expense to the P.T.T. Was I really SURE that I should object to that little wire?

I remained smiling but adamant:

"*Je regrette, Monsieur — !*"

He gave an expressive Gallic shrug, once more exposed his strong white tombstone teeth in a rueful grin, shook my hand warmly, and departed with an English cigarette to comfort him. Downstairs he remarked to Henri and Louise that *Madame* had been too quick for them. In another half-hour that wire would have been placed across her property and, once there, would have remained — for some long time — even if she had told the Authorities to remove it! *Madame* knew this full well, and was very grateful to her Gazelle for warning her in time.

One makes friends among the telephone operators at the Exchange. There are certain efficient women whose voices I have learned to know — one, especially, with a deep husky and most attractive contralto voice, who quietly and politely asks me what number I want and gets it for me, a relief after sometimes wasting ten minutes or so with some feckless young maiden whose silly gossip can easily be heard as she interrupts her conversation with her neighbour to ask me what number I want. I tell her and wait while she presses invisible switches, continuing her giggling conversation with her friend while I am given the wrong number, of course. Then we begin all over again.

But I always enjoy my conversations in the evening because then a dear old beaver is in charge of the telephone. I have never seen him, but I know he's an old beaver, for his voice has lost the timbre of youth and he speaks as through fur. He is also slightly deaf, but most courteous and persevering. He never snaps at me and never once has he given me the wrong number or caused me any of the irritation or annoyance that I must surely often have given him. He is a prince of beavers, and his splendid service did not fail when once I was obliged to ask him to get me a number in England. I did it reluctantly; for I know him to be single-handed at night and I felt that a call to Berkhamstead might break his unvarying patience. It did not. I had to spell that awful place-name in the French manner and he got it at once. He is leisurely but sure. One day when I sense that he is not overburdened with incoming and outgoing calls, on Sunday perhaps, I shall introduce myself as a person and not merely a voice and shall ask him his name, even perhaps his age. Afterwards our telephonic communications will become cosy, for I shall tell him how much I look forward to his advent in the evening and how greatly I appreciate his courtesy. It should prove a good example to the younger operators — only unfortunately they are not there to profit by it.

CHAPTER EIGHT

We Entertain

We, in the South of France, who with our small incomes prefer to live in the little hill-towns and villages up in the mountains above Cannes, Grasse and Nice, have made post-war hospitality a fine art. Although with only a limited domestic staff — generally consisting of a *bonne-à-tout-faire*, and a gardener who does anything and everything not included in his horticultural work — we yet contrive to entertain our friends and vie with each other to give a "different" party with some touch of originality about it. But it is an understood thing that if a would-be hostess is short of cutlery, crockery, glasses — or staff — she at once rings up one or other of her invited guests, begs her to arrive early, bringing with her extra knives, plates, or whatever may be most wanted, and very often her *bonne*, chauffeur or gardener to help with the service if the party has swollen since its inception:

"Darling! Will you bring your Yvonne with you to help my *bonne*? You'll be eating here, so she will have nothing to do at home — and can you bring six wine glasses? I thought I had enough, but everyone seems to be bringing one or more house-guests with them, and now there's no time to rush down to Cannes and buy more at the *Monoprix*" (the French equivalent of Woolworths, haunted by the English residents).

The reply is always in the affirmative, with generally a few more generous suggestions.

"Of course I'll bring Yvonne; she'll adore it. And do you want extra food? I've got some American tins. You could have a Paysandu tongue, a whole chicken, butter, coffee. Oh! What should we do without those American parcels?"

I shall always remember my last birthday party at "Sunset House" before the war. Not only did my guests bring with them beautiful gifts for me, but they also supplied deficiencies of food and service.

Old Phillips Oppenheim, a near neighbour, came rolling across my courtyard carrying a magnum of champagne. In his wake came his dear little wife, Elsie, holding a lovely silvered basket of lilies-of-the-valley (my flower), while bringing up the rear pattered their excellent *Maître d'Hôtel*, who at once took charge of preliminary cocktails, thereafter serving luncheon. And, though he had never been in my house before, he found everything necessary and never made a mistake, which seemed to me almost miraculous.

A little Russian princess and her English husband provided the most wonderful basket of fruit for dessert, arranged with the inimitable artistry of the French; someone else brought salted nuts of every rare species, also *marrons glacés* and chocolate truffles. My *bonne* surpassed herself in the kitchen, making use of our poultry and tender fresh vegetables, but it was my guests who supplied the luxurious extras which I should not have been justified in buying at such fantastic prices.

Our American visitors find amusement when they entertain their friends in hired houses in Provence. One of them, who tenanted *Mademoiselle's Château* for a few weeks, invited two Oil Queens to stay with him. His staff, chiefly composed of our local peasants, could never grasp the names of these ladies and when speaking of them to me referred to them as *Madame* Shell and *Madame* Mobiloil, to the great joy of their host, to whom I confided their nicknames.

It is new to them to be pressed to help themselves more liberally of the contents of a dish presented to them by the *bonne* who prepared it, these invitations usually accompanied by comments upon the too thin or too fat proportions of the person being tempted to eat. A thin lady must eat more to obtain those curves pleasing to gentlemen, and a fat husband must eat well to increase his generous proportions, because it is well known that you can't have too much of a good thing and he will keep his wife warmer in bed in winter.

Sophisticated servants are trained to silent service, and my guests are sometimes startled when their conversation at table is suddenly interrupted by Louise's hyena laugh when, from gesture, she grasps what they are saying, and by the noisy slapping of her thighs when something amuses her. But they can seldom resist her kindness, her humour, and her delight if she be referred to for advice or be cosily included in the conversation.

Since the war our parties have become more and more communal, and it is delightful to be sure of the support of one's friends without which, in these difficult days, one would never have the courage to entertain.

My loveliest party this year was given to eighty Naval Ratings of the British Mediterranean Fleet.

Last year our Consul voiced a plea that English residents in the Riviera should give hospitality to junior officers when the ships should come in. He said that the midshipmen, who sleep in hammocks, would so appreciate having a night or two in a comfortable bed and feeling that they could leave a litter of possessions and clothes on the floor if they liked, without fear of reproof from a Senior Officer.

For some reason or other I was then unable to offer my one little guest-room, but this year I kept it free for one midshipman, and also said I would love to give a party for the Naval Ratings, as everyone tried to snaffle officers and the blue-jackets were excluded from private houses. Several *char-à-banc* expeditions were always arranged for the men, but there were blank days when one saw them perched moodily on walls or trying to sell cigarettes to enable them to buy souvenirs for their women-folk or a glass of beer for themselves in a *bistro*. They looked bored and lost, and I felt sure would appreciate a welcome in an English home. I told the Consul that *if* it was a fine day I could cope with two *char-à-banc* loads — about eighty men — as they could overflow into the garden and olive grove when my little house was crowded.

I rather wondered whether a day up in our mountains might bore the men, but one of their officers told me that the list of applicants for my party far exceeded eighty, and that a great many had to be disappointed.

When the day had been fixed I rang up every member of the British and American Colony of the neighbourhood asking them all to come and help me to receive my guests AND to bring a contribution of food or drink for my hungry and thirsty multitude. I suggested that the men should bring beer and the women cakes or sandwiches. This was before I found Louise, and I had a temporary and temperamental *bonne*, who had a sister in Grasse, by trade a confectioner. She begged me to let her go home for one afternoon before the party. Afterwards I heard that she had prepared her departure, armed with every sort of kitchen utensil and dish, not to mention bags of (American) flour and, as it seemed to me when endless bills were presented for payment after the event, all the available eggs of the neighbourhood. Being unable to drag this mass of material to the local motor bus, she begged me to allow my niece, who was staying with me, to drive her to Grasse in the little *Peugeot Camionette*. My midshipman guest, agog for adventure, insisted upon accompanying the niece and my *bonne*, although this had meant that he must almost sit on the crates of eggs in the back of the little car. In this broody position he assured me that he had been able to guard all the china bowls and other implements as the car jolted over the stony mountain road, particularly uneven at this moment as a torrential rain had washed away the surface and uncovered ledges of bare rock.

Their journey proved to be amusing, but I do not think the dear boy found it so funny to drag all that heavy stuff up steep flights of stairs to the fifth floor where my *bonne* had a tiny flat. Why she would not invite her sister to come here and make her miracles of *patisserie* in my modern kitchen remains a partial mystery to me, but I imagine that it was more fun to work amid admiring friends in the town of Grasse, running in and out of neighbour's houses and sipping *apéritifs* while the town baker made the cakes. There would also be the triumphal progress through the crowded streets to the baker's abode, and much boasting to the populace about the marvellous reception *Madame* was giving to the British Fleet.

Rumours of this, distasteful to me, floated back to my quiet little mountain home after the event. I hate pretension. I am not a rich woman, and I had told my *bonne* that I would supply split rolls, buttered and lined with ham, the butter and ham gifts from America. This form of French sandwich is filling and always popular, especially when eaten with beer. But my *bonne*, anxious to "make a splash" and to advertise her art, had planned a surprise for *Madame*, who was to know nothing about it until THE day. At the time I only knew that the *Peugeot* was to drive her into Grasse.

There followed the usual spuffle of preparations which must always precede a "party" in a small house. Somewhere — WHERE? — I had an enormous Union Jack stored away, together with the Stars and Stripes and the *Tricolor* of France. I had bought them in England to celebrate the Peace when it should come, and so enormous were they that they had almost covered my tiny cottage in the Sussex woods. These must certainly be found and the ladder to the loft perilously ascended; trunks and suitcases stored there were opened and searched, and eventually my flags were thrown joyfully down from the trap-door to the Studio below. We then rehearsed effects. The huge Union Jack should be suspended from my little square tower to guide my guests to the house and give the right welcome. A small one should be hung outside the entrance gates, and the American flag, flanked by two French *tricolors* would decorate the outside of my loggia facing the courtyard entrance. Henri, beaming and sweating with pride, rehearsed these effects while we criticised from the road, and found them to be excellent.

The patriotic note having been struck, I turned my attention to crockery, and extracted the harlequin selection of cups and plates of broken-up tea-sets, reserving the only service left intact for the use of my helpers, who would also need refreshment. Every tumbler was brought forth — pitifully few left to me since the war — but I had implored the officer who was organising this outing to order the men each to bring his own mug (I forget the naval word for a mug) as I could never provide eighty receptacles for beer and tea.

The great day dawned, grey skies but mercifully no rain. I had been haunted by dread thoughts of a wet day, for my little dining-hall, communicating through a wide square aperture with the tiny *salon*, had just held thirty-three people for my Christmas buffet-dinner, using both rooms, and I had now invited at least a hundred! If fine, the men could sit on the grass of the little lawns and on the terraces of the olive grove, but, oh! IF WET . . .

I had anticipated, as I thought, all the crises which could occur before the arrival of my guests. The electricity might be cut; the Butagaz cylinder might be exhausted just when we needed kettles of boiling water for making tea; my helpers might forget to bring the promised supplementary supplies of food and drink or, coming from afar as some of them were, and perhaps combining a luncheon engagement elsewhere on the same day, might arrive long after the sailors. And the sailors would be both hungry and thirsty, for they were being taken first to visit one of the *Parfumeries* in Grasse, and then up to Gourdon, perched on its precipitous peak, with a marvellous panorama of the surrounding landscape far, far below.

I had *not* anticipated the most serious mishap that could befall me.

I was eating a hurried tray-lunch in my Studio when Henri battered on the outside door. He had just been warned that half the supporting wall of my road to the *Domaine* had fallen down during that morning, the result of spring rains. If those huge *char-à-bancs* attempted to approach the house by this route the whole road would surely collapse, and the motor coaches with their precious load of British sailors would roll down into the olive groves of *Monsieur* Pagani, "*Quel désastre!*" Yes, indeed, it would be a disaster, and if I were to avert it I must act quickly, because I had told our British Consul, who was to accompany the sailors and show them the way to my house, that the coaches could easily travel down that road and turn outside the gates of my *Domaine*. A huge Army truck filled with crates of food for the children of Provence had already performed this feat, driven by a baby American Quaker.

The only thing to do was for my large Henri to thunder down the lane to the main road and stop the *char-à-bancs* before they turned into it. But he would have to be quick about it, for they were almost due to arrive.

With what relief did I see the blue-jackets, led by the Consul's wife, marching towards my gates!

The second unforeseen crisis was when I discovered that only *one* of the eighty had remembered to bring his mug! However, my helpers had arrived early as promised, the women laden with boxes and trays of delicious cakes, sandwiches and rolls, and the men with crates of beer.

I had put one of the men in the little sun-porch outside my *salon* to act as barman, and seeing my despair about the non-existent mugs, he said:

"But there are enough bottles of beer for each man to have at least a bottle apiece. They'll quaff the precious fluid from the bottle — and be enchanted!"

They were. After greeting them all, I cried: "This way to the Beer Bar," and there was a general rush in the direction indicated by my pointing finger. Soon my terraces and walls were decorated with happy blue-jackets, each one sucking at his bottle of beer. My helpers carried out the trays of buns, sandwiches, cakes, rolls, and hard-boiled eggs. The *pièces de resistance* were three enormous pewter plates decorated with red, white, and blue flowers. On these were mountainously piled my *bonne's* "surprise," towering pyramids of *brioches glacés* filled with vanilla cream and posed upon great circular cakes. No wonder she needed FOURTEEN DOZEN EGGS to make these miracles of confectionery! She got all the praise and admiration her soul craved, and no doubt I have now the reputation of being a millionairess and my bills will mount accordingly. *My* reward was when she came to me next day and said she had strained a shoulder muscle turning around the mass of *pâte* to make these cakes; and now she must go home and rest for some long time, as *Madame* had killed her with overwork!

However while the blue-jackets were with me nothing spoiled that happy afternoon. And it was a happy afternoon; for those men did appreciate being received into an English home and being made so welcome. Some of my helpers had feared, as I had, that our guests would be bored, since I had nothing save peace, beauty, and refreshments to offer them in this lovely but isolated corner of Provence, but I suppose that we had all momentarily forgotten the things most of those men had lived through during the war: bombs from the air, torpedoes and mines from the sea, and discomfort everywhere. This quiet afternoon might be very welcome to many. Anyhow those dear men seemed to like clambering about my walls and up my stone stairways, and seeing the little grotto chapel in the rock under the house, where two English babies have been baptised. I think, above all things, they enjoyed climbing on to the roof-terrace of my little square tower, for it commands a marvellous view. I told them I had installed a *douche* for sun-bathers on my roof, and they were vastly amused at the story of the awful evening in 1939 when an important French General and his two A.D.C.s came to dinner with me and asked to see the surrounding landscape from my tower by moonlight. The tap which controls the *douche* is hidden behind the door leading out on to the terrace. Wishing to demonstrate the working of the cooling system to the young A.D.C.s I turned it on — not knowing the General was standing immediately under the *douche* — !

I soused him well, that poor General, and his two A.D.C.s had to turn their backs and rush to the parapet stifling irreverent laughter. *I* nearly bit a hole in my cheek striving to control mine as I dried him. Luckily he, also, had a sense of humour.

I seemed doomed to water French Generals. Another one called upon me, and seeing that the great bell which hangs outside the gateway had got stuck in an upside-down position, rashly pulled its rope — it had been raining hard and the inverted bell was full of water.

Water misfortunes are usually amusing, and the sailors found out the truth of this on that spring afternoon if they didn't know it before. My niece, who had thoroughly enjoyed my stories about the Generals, having, like her aunt, a large spice of gamine in her, showed parties of sailors the working of the *douche*. One of them, with devils in his eyes, then hid behind the door and soused each succeeding sailor as he stepped out on to the roof-terrace. He also forbore to warn his friends that the doorway was low and that there was danger of bumped heads. Meanwhile I was sitting in the

Studio talking to blue-jackets overflowing chairs and divan and sitting in circles around me on the floor. Our hilarity was drowned by yells and execrations from overhead. Suddenly a large body tobogganed down the steep stairway and arrived on its bottom on the floor of my Studio. "They've found out it's me that's been soakin' them," it gasped between bursts of laughter, "and they're after me!"

The practical joker scrambled to his feet and made good his escape, as a torrent of damp and chuckling sailors cascaded down that dangerous little staircase in vengeful pursuit.

These aquatic and gymnastic sports enlivened the afternoon considerably, and when my guests had swilled down large cups of tea we all said regretful farewells; for a Kill-Joy had looked at his watch and said it was time to regain their ship.

Next morning Henri came to me with a worried look.

"La chaine de cabinet en bas manque, Madame," he ejaculated with a puzzled voice.

The chain of the downstairs lavatory was missing. And then I remembered that our midshipman guest had told us that such souvenirs were collected by the men (*and* by the junior officers) and hung as trophies in gun-rooms and messes. Doubtless that practical joker was also the thief of this treasure of the *Domaine*. Anyway, as a result of that joyous afternoon I lost my *bonne* (I did NOT weep) and a nice nickel chain.

Picnics here are very popular, each person bringing his or her own food to be pooled, and there is great rivalry among us over who will be able to produce the first-fruits of the year; for we work hard in our gardens and are very proud of the produce, heartening our gardeners to grow *primeurs*.

Gardening here becomes a fine art, for the soil varies on every terrace. One finds a pocket of clay next to a sandy patch. One tries to dig a hole for the planting of a fruit tree and comes upon solid rock which only dynamite will dislodge. Our first *Domaine* was blessed by entirely fertile soil in which everything we planted prospered exceedingly, and we were obliged to steal or buy rocks to make a rock-garden. Here, with the exception of a few tracts of fairly good soil which must nevertheless be enriched, we have rock.

This year, for some reason, about eighty of my vines wilted and died, in spite of Henri's meticulous care. Completely puzzled, for they showed no sign of *la maladie* against which he had sedulously sprayed them, Henri proceeded to dig one up. He discovered that the peasant who had planted them had only removed a certain amount of rock — evidently a lazy man who hoped that the quantity of soil he had freed from rock would be enough to nourish the vines during his lifetime. Well — they had reached bed-rock in mine.

It was during that hectic week of cherry-picking that this discovery was made and, I learned afterwards, Henri had a bad bout of toothache. For the first time since I have known him he lost his smile and became irritable. He even bit *me*.

He was working in the vegetable garden during that untimely period of hot weather. I had been ill for some weeks and at last was allowed by my doctor to get up and make a little tour of the garden. Knowing that poor Henri must be having a hard time digging ground so parched that it was almost as hard as the rock beneath it, I decided that my first wobbly walk must be in his direction to administer the encouragement he deserved and must sorely need.

He was bending down as I approached, the reinforced patch on his blue working trousers very much in evidence.

I asked him cheerily what he was doing, and instead of straightening his huge frame and turning upon me a beaming face to tell me how glad he was to see me up and out again, to my astonishment he merely looked at me between his legs with a furious upside-down face and muttered something quite unintelligible. He never has clear diction, partly because of his teeth, and this was before he was finally driven to the dentist. Even the Gazelle, though she can understand every other peasant, admits that she missed more than half of Henri's conversation. Now I could not understand one word he muttered in reply.

So I repeated my inquiry, and it seemed to enrage him. Wheeling upon me, his countenance empurpled, he positively roared:

"ARROSAGE! ARROSAGE!"

I was so taken aback by his abrupt rudeness that my weak knees gave under me and I sank down, amazed and confounded, upon a convenient wall.

Then he relented somewhat, and explained that the ground was so hard that when he tried to irrigate his vegetables the water could not sink into the soil, but ran straight down into the road beneath. He had emptied a 20,000 *litre bassin* that afternoon and had done no good at all, so now was obliged to dig hollows around each vegetable and pour water into them. No wonder he was exasperated! and when I heard torrential rain falling in the night I positively did not dare the next day to face my poor Henri, whose toil had been for nothing.

It will be seen that gardeners in the South of France have much to contend with, so that if one of them can produce early lettuces, peas, and haricot beans before his rival gardener next door he is a proud man and his employer shares his glory. It gives a glow when, on unpacking one's picnic basket to display ripe cherries, one hears a chorus of "Cherries! *Yours?* Mine aren't half ripe yet. How lucky you are to have cherries so early."

I wonder from whence the love and the art of eating out-of-doors came to the English — to be perfected by Americans. Men and women of other nations seldom go for picnics, but prefer to enjoy their meals comfortably in their homes or in restaurants, but we have turned *al fresco* meals into a fine art.

The famous Elizabeth Russell — Elizabeth of the German Garden — adored bathing and a picnic lunch on the shore afterwards. It always consisted of a hot-pot of mutton and vegetables which one spooned out of a gigantic Thermos flask. Queer fare in broiling summer weather under a hot sun, but she preferred it to all else, partly because it saved so much trouble to have one's meal concentrated in this way, for the only extra required was a hunk of bread. I shared many of these picnics with her, but the most memorable was at Théoule, when Ernest Shepard, of "Punch" fame, was staying with me to get sketches for the illustrations for my book "Perfume from Provence," and I shall ever have a vision of the tiny Elizabeth bobbing up and down in the sea — she couldn't swim or float, but loved thus to refresh herself, looking up coquettishly into the face of the tall, thin Kip Shepard, who looked like a stick of peppermint rock in his striped swimming-suit, as she uttered her daring witticisms. After the bathe, Mary Shepard, radiant and plump in a rather revealing backless bathing-dress (which to-day would seem positively prudish) asked me if I thought that Lady Russell would mind if she ate her luncheon thus attired. Knowing my Elizabeth and the curious streak of formality in her — perhaps derived from her life in Germany as the Gräfin von Arnhim — I suggested that it would perhaps be better to ask her. Accordingly Mary approached the tent where Elizabeth was dressing and inquired: "Lady Russell, do you mind if I lunch in my swimming-suit?"

After a pause, Elizabeth's little voice replied rather coldly: "No, I suppose not, my dear — if *you* do not mind." Whereupon Mary, with a little grin, cast herself down upon the sand by my side in an abandonment of grace and youthful curves which were glanced over somewhat icily by Elizabeth's blue eyes when she emerged from the tent.

So that, sensing her disapproval of Mary, I was staggered when her good-looking *chauffeur*, Jean, appeared to serve our luncheon clad in only the briefest pair of trunks — to-day I believe described as *cache-sexe*.

How I miss little Elizabeth Russell! Her tongue was sharp and her wit often mordant, but what a loyal friend she was to me and how often did her deliciously unexpected remarks refresh me during my Man's long illness. Every day she telephoned for news of him, and on one occasion when I was able to give her a good report she said:

"Oh, Peggy! How you must be thanking God." A pause, and then with a laugh: "Now *I* am always thanking God that all my husbands (she had had but two) are dead."

There was another pause, and finally came this profound remark:

"When you think of it, darling, God must get thanked for almost everything."

I loved going to see her in her *Mas des Roses* in Mougins. She had covered her walls everywhere with pink climbing roses of every variety (mostly supplied by me from cuttings taken from the English roses which John and I ordered in 1931 before the ban on export), and her terraces were lined with mauve Pallida iris, so that she was surrounded by pastel shades, which suited well her blonde hair and skin. Elizabeth had great dramatic sense. Her clothes and her setting were always right, and only inside her Studio in the garden did she seat herself anywhere save among cushions of pale French brocade. There she would perch before a large desk in a truly enormous chair, once the property of Frederick the Great — a von Arnhim family treasure — while she wrote her immortal books, her little legs dangling in the air, for she was a tiny person.

Her *salon* was always filled with intelligent people, chiefly men, whom she held enthralled and fascinated by her sometimes cruel wit and her charm. She was always talking of giving a *Fête Champêtre* in her garden by moonlight, and I heard her one day trying to persuade Edwina Stuart-Wortley, "Louise" of opera fame, to sing for her in this romantic setting. Edwina very wisely refused. She had not sung in public for years, her voice might crack or she might perhaps sing out of tune.

"But you'd be singing in the dark, my dear," persisted the tactless little Elizabeth, and Edwina rolled laughing eyes at me, then heavenward.

What an outrageous remark to make to an artist!

That *Fête Champêtre* never came off, but I attended the loveliest one the other day given by the most talented and versatile man of our English Colony. He planned for it to take place in his lovely grounds, a green valley set amid the pine-woods that crown the low hills surrounding his property, and through which flows a gentle little river flanked by weeping willows. Near his house, which is built on the site of an old olive mill, is the cascade that once turned the mill-wheel, and below it the quiet river is dammed to form a miniature weir so that always one hears the refreshing sound of falling water.

At that date the moon was full. Our host had made the condition that everyone invited should wear Greek or Roman classical attire. He gave us greeting draped in a sheet of apricot *crêpe-de-chine*, his own white hair gilded with metal paint (which was an agony to remove afterwards) and arranged in classical undulations by an expert coiffeur. He looked a very noble Roman Senator.

I had been ill for months and was still far from strong, but I knew that this *Fête* would be an artistic triumph and I longed to see it. I had had no time or energy to plan and have fitted a new dress, and I knew I was not strong enough to walk about the grounds for hours, for my host could not possibly seat the multitude of his guests.

Then inspiration came, supplied by the old poet Ben Jonson. I would wear my white satin evening dress, which is draped in Greek fashion with long scarves. Being made of artificial silk (because cheaper) the material shines with an odd brilliance and would gleam in the moonlight. I could represent Diana, Goddess of the Moon: —

> "Queen and Huntress chaste and fair
> Now the sun is laid to sleep
> Seated in thy silver chair
>
> State in wonted manner keep . . ."

I would paint a garden chair with aluminium paint, and somehow make a huge crescent moon to fix to its back so that I would seem to be seated in the moon. And I would contrive to design a large silver full moon to wear as a halo for my head — the moon with a face looking out of it. To this I would attach yards and yards

of white tulle sewn at intervals with silver sequined stars
— if I could find any — to represent a cloud.

If I took my own chair with me I should be assured of
a seat, and could enjoy a lovely evening at the cost of
some ingenuity, a few yards of tulle, and a pot of silver
paint. The Gazelle and her mother, who was then staying
with me, must also be attired, and after long searchings
of classical dictionaries, books of Greek mythology, and
so on, we decided that the Gazelle should represent the
Goddess Flora and wear one of my long draped
tea-gowns of *mousseline-de-soie* in sweet-pea colourings
(chosen by *Monsieur* in 1914!), mauve over a deep rose
pink, and a coronet, girdle, and bracelet of real flowers.
Her mother, who has the loveliest serene expression,
would represent the Goddess of Peace, and wear one of
my white winged tea-gowns, looped up with silver
ribbon — she is shorter than I — with sprays of olive
branches binding her hair and a large branch in her
hand.

If only I could somehow construct a dove of peace to
sit upon her shoulder! And here Louise came in. She had
condemned to death by Henri an ancient white hen,
destined for the pot, and, quite unknown to me (upon
this I always insist), the massacre took place on the
morning of the *Fête*. When she found me in my Studio
smeared all over with silver paint, Henri with sweat
literally pouring from his brow in drops upon the
pale-grey tiles as he valiantly endeavoured to hack out a
crescent moon from extremely stiff cardboard, the
Gazelle surrounded by cut flowers and olive branches,
and her mother laughing at our efforts amid such

144

picturesque chaos; and heard me bewail my inability to provide white feathers with which to fabricate a Dove of Peace, she rushed precipitately from the room and presently returned in triumph with a handful of feathers plucked from her victim in the kitchen.

With these "Mummie" constructed the dove. It was the oddest Dove of Peace I ever beheld, symbolic perhaps of the extremely queer peace we have enjoyed since 1945.

In the end, after much agony — amusing agony — we really were quite an effective trio as we drove off by moonlight to that memorable *Fête Champêtre classique au clair de lune*.

My silver chair was placed at a point of vantage by my kind host under a giant umbrella'd plane tree, from where I could survey the scene all around me, lit by fairy lamps and swinging Chinese lanterns, and watch shadowy classical figures wandering amid the flowers like a dream of the past come to life again in that Happy Valley. As I sat enthroned, my whimsical fancy could not help trying to picture what had taken place behind the scenes in each individual house to achieve such costumes; what linen-cupboards had been ransacked to produce sheets which could be draped into togas and tunics; the multitude of safety-pins employed to fix them into suitable folds upon the torsos of impatient and self-conscious males; the fishmongers' shops which had been scoured to provide scallop shells to adorn Neptune and his band of Tritons; the toy-shops which had been searched to find mechanical snakes to decorate the head of the bewigged stout American gentleman who represented Medusa and who inadvertently stepped back into a *rigole* of water, losing both his balance and his wig, which he hastily fished for and replaced at a drunken angle upon his head, each snake uncoiled and dripping water over his ample draperies.

Whatever the home complications, the results achieved were quite lovely, seen by the light of the moon, and the Bengal flares and fireworks provided as a surprise by the little French laundryman of our host.

The *grand finale* was at midnight, when a huge bonfire was lit in the field in front of the house, and goddesses, gods, fauns, dryads, and satyrs danced around it wildly to the strains of a gypsy band, whose players capered in an outer circle playing violins, guitars, and accordions.

A mad Greek frieze come to life.

CHAPTER
NINE

New Year in Provence

In England, Christmas is the great feast for old and young alike, but in France it is only for the children, who put out their little *sabots* on Christmas Eve before going to bed, hoping that *Papa Noël* will fill them with exciting presents during the night. It is the New Year that is fêted by everybody in France. Shops are filled with *étrennes* of every description, lovely gifts of perfume, *bon-bons*, handbags, jewellery, and flowers. The buyers are sure that their purchases will be packed up ready for presentation with the true artistry of the French, enveloped in papers of every delicate hue, tied with rainbow ribbons and sealed with butterflies, birds or *cigales* in gold, silver, green, or blue. Flowers will not be just bunched but exquisitely arranged, as are the interiors of boxes of *bon-bons*; chocolates interspersed with crystallised violets, rose-petals, yellow bobbles of mimosa, tiny oranges and lemons, and very often some sentimental verse about Love and Friendship scrolled delicately upon the lid. On New Year's Eve there is feverish activity in all the shops and markets, everyone buying food for *le Reveillon* feast and last-minute *étrennes* (New Year gifts). Even the policemen on point

147

duty standing upon their little platforms are surrounded by circles of gift-bottles of wine. I proferred mine to the handsome beaming *gendarme* as I passed him last year in my little car, and he bent down to receive it as I thrust it through the window: "*Merci, Madame! Mes meilleurs vœux pour une bonne année,*" he said as he added it to his collection. Then, seeing a too-hilarious driver backing his car at a reckless pace from the Car Park without waiting for the signal, the *gendarme* yelled: "*Imbécile! Que faîtes-vous là?*" and blew shrilly on his whistle, commanding the evil-doer to stop.

The *Imbécile* successfully turned his car, with great inconvenience and danger to everybody, but fortunately causing no casualties, drew up obediently beside the *gendarme's* platform, and stifled reproof swiftly and tactfully by thrusting a magnum of champagne under his nose.

"*Merci, Monsieur! Vous êtes bien amiable!*" and the fierce frown of outraged authority was replaced by the widest smile.

As I watched I couldn't help wishing that when I was doing my New Year's shopping in Nice I had provided myself with a propitiatory bottle of wine to hand in like manner to an enraged *gendarme*.

I was driving in my little Baby Austin, known here as "*Le petit pigeon gris,*" down that terrifying *Avenue de la Victoire*, which is always filled with surging traffic, intensified a hundredfold at this season of the year. I wanted information as to the locality of a certain street, so I manœuvred my little car (which, being English, has the driving-wheel on the right side) to get alongside the *gendarme* on point duty at the end of the *Avenue*.

I thought I had judged the distance correctly, but as, in France, one drives on the right side of the road it is really better and safer to lean across and put one's head out of the window on the left side when performing such a manœuvre. This I did not do, and as I approached the *gendarme* the little car gave a lurch which was followed by a terrified spate of angry abuse from the *gendarme*. I had driven onto the edge of the little wooden safety platform from which my *gendarme* was perched to control the traffic — !

Luckily my little car weighs nothing at all or its weight might have tipped up that platform and deposited the *gendarme* on its bonnet.

I asked for *no* instructions. Fortunately for me the traffic lights were in my favour and the congestion of vehicles so great that the *gendarme* had hard work to control it. I accelerated furiously and his blast of abuse speeded me on my way. I FLED before he had time to regain his breath to blow that whistle which must be obeyed, and so, by a miracle, I escaped a *contravention*, for to endanger the life of a policeman must be a heinous offence.

Had I been armed with a magnum of champagne that *gendarme* and I would have parted on kissing instead of hissing terms.

Of course I told this story against myself to all my friends and I shall never hear the last of it. That I, who have driven a car since 1918 and never once had a summons, I who possess an unblemished record and a driving licence without one endorsement, should endanger this by assaulting a *gendarme* on his sacred platform is too good a story to be soon forgotten.

It would be most undignified for an officer of the law to be carried off on the bonnet of a car, but it *could* happen.

Once, in St Tropez, during such a terrific mistral that the sea was washed over the edge of the port and flooded the streets, when tiles and barrows, fruit baskets, sun-umbrellas, fishing nets and tackle whirled through the air, *Mademoiselle* and I were obliged to go into the town on a shopping expedition.

I drew up my car in the main interior street but opposite a narrow one which led to the port, and there awaited *Mademoiselle*, who went into a sheltered shop. Suddenly — you will find it hard to believe — a little French sailor came hurtling through the air and landed on the bonnet of my car. He had been blown off his feet by that tremendous wind and whirled down the narrow side-street from the port and came to anchor there. I have never before seen such a surprised sailor. I, also, received somewhat of a shock. We looked at each other in a dazed manner — and then we both began to laugh. When he had regained his breath, completely blown out of him by the mistral, he slid off the bonnet and came round to the window saying:

"*Je vous demande pardon, Madame, mais ce vent est plus fort que moi!*"

New Year cards replace the delicious sparklers of Christmas, which depict flights of baby angels surrounding the crib of the Holy Babe lying in a snow-covered stable, or the Christ Child bestriding a miniature donkey riding through an open gate into a snow-covered world, followed by a host of cherubs, just rosy faces and sparkling wings — the same made magical and glorious by the powdered frosted glass pasted on the surface. I send away these cards because my English friends love them, but always I long to keep them for myself. The New Year cards are more sophisticated and sparkle less; sprays of flowers under which is written *Bonne Année* and other greetings, but always they accompany some delicious gift.

France goes a bit mad at the New Year. Families entertain lavishly; the French, usually, *en hôtels*, the English and American residents in their own houses, and every *Casino* has its Gala. I had the felicity of having a very young and lovely little niece staying with me one New Year before the war. To her everything was the most tremendous thrill. As a child, her mother had brought her out to me, and even at that tender age the beauty of Provence intoxicated her. She gazed at our lilac and purple mountains under a flaming sunset sky of orange and rose and palest Nile green with blue eyes wide with ecstasy, and when we drove up to a higher altitude and she could fill the skirt of her little frock with *wild* miniature iris and pheasant-eyed narcissi, on her return she blew up a temperature and babbled of flowers all night in her feverish sleep.

Now she was seventeen, but just as impressionable and completely unspoiled. I took her to a Gala in Cannes. We sat with a large and distinguished party of people, clever men and bejewelled women with their faces exquisitely made up and their beautiful nails enamelled to match their lips, but my child, clad in a simple bouffant picture dress of black taffeta secured over her milk-white immature shoulders by narrow straps, her heart-shaped face faintly flushed with excitement, the pupils of her huge blue eyes dilated and her fluffy, wavy, silvery gold hair forming an aureole around that angelic little face, guiltless of cosmetics, wearing no jewels or flowers — herself a wild flower needing no adornment — outshone them all.

During dinner I noticed my child rolling apprehensive eyes around her when presented with some difficult and unknown dish to see how others had dealt with it — so deliciously young. At the end the usual scenic effect was produced by the Management of *L'Ambassadeurs*. Suddenly the room was darkened and showers of scintillating (artificial) rain-drops poured down the windows, lit invisibly by multi-coloured lights, like chains of diamonds, rose, yellow, green, and then a lovely unearthly blue. I was sitting next to a very famous retired Parisian specialist, beloved and much sought-after by the English because of his brilliant brain, extraordinary charm, and French wit. When that blue blaze lit the room he seized my arm. Turning to him I saw his eyes riveted upon my little niece. She sat entranced, her head thrown back, every faint vein in her slender neck delicately revealed, lips parted, eyes wide and her hair turned to silver in that blue glare, looking almost too lovely and etherial to be real. Around her those mondaine women were shamed by that blue light which turned their painted faces into grotesque masks. I heard the doctor mutter, his eyes still riveted on my child:

"Si j'avais vingt-cinq ans!"

I call her "my" child, because having none of my very own, though I always longed for at least eighteen (to be born preferably in twos and threes so that I didn't have to wait too long for my family to augment) my sister promised that if she had two babies she would give me one of them. She produced only one, this lovely child, so I had to have half of her.

We two went also to the great Carnival at Nice. My Fay saw the Battle of Flowers, with its procession of flower-decked carriages, cars and chariots, and in the evening we attended the Gala at the Hotel Negresco. For dinner the *Maître d'Hôtel*, who, being a swarthy Latin, needless to say had fallen flat for this transparent blonde, suggested that *Mademoiselle* would perhaps like a table where she could see the band. See the band? I always imagined that one listened to a band, and to be near the one hundred jazz musicians advertised to entertain us — Ray Ventura and his orchestra — would be, to me, a foretaste of hell. If my food must be accompanied by music, I prefer a soft DISTANT string band. But how could I resist those pleading radiant blue eyes with their expression of intense supplication? She had heard of the famous Ray Ventura. I, being I suppose moss-grown, never had, and so, with difficulty, we were given a table in the fourth row, at the back of the room but fairly near the orchestra. When it began to play I realised that the *Maître d'Hôtel had* used the right word "see" the orchestra; for, once they began to play,

153

every member of it seemed to go mad. To the accompaniment of the ghastly noise they were making they performed incredible contortions and acrobatic feats which positively thrilled the child. Before the evening was over she had somehow secured the promise of an enormous photograph signed by Ray Ventura and every member of his orchestra, and it is still one of her proud possessions.

After this sensational overture the ever-solicitous *Maître d'Hôtel* sidled up to us and made another suggestion. The *Cabaret* from Paris was about to begin, and perhaps *Mademoiselle* would see it better if she stood upon a table, for the crowd of spectators would thicken and many of them would be standing up. With his eager aid and much alacrity *Mademoiselle* clambered upon his proferred table, the lights were lowered, and the show began.

The artists were selected from *Les Folies Bergères*, and those who have frequented that place of amusement will not be as surprised as I was when a lady as nude as she very well could be — I think she wore a scarf of gauze — glided from between velvet curtains.

My niece was even more stupefied than I. Clasping frail white hands she exclaimed in a shrill and extremely audible voice of delighted horror, with blue eyes positively goggling: "Auntie Win! SHE HASN'T GOT A STITCH ON!"

Two sophisticated Frenchmen strolling past looked up at her as though they would like to eat this delicious Innocent. Her spontaneous remark had a *succès fou* with that audience of blasé people and made the evening for me.

The Gazelle had never before crossed the sea when she came out to Opio and so was thrilled by everything. Everyone in the world has heard of the great annual Carnival at Nice, and very naturally she longed to see it. I warned her that she might be disappointed, as I had been, though of course I saw it at a more advanced age. I had imagined lovely masked ladies in multi-coloured dominoes tripping about the streets pursued discreetly by mysterious masked men who threw bunches of violets and bouquets of carnations to the unknown beauties who attracted them. But gone were these ancient customs, and romance had been succeeded by rowdyism, flowers by confetti, which fell in showers everywhere and was scooped up from the gutters to be thrown again, or, best joke of all, stuffed into the mouths of laughing maidens by the roughs of the town. An old doctor here told me that after the Carnival he usually had to deal with many cases of diphtheria caused by this.

But my Gazelle was in no way deterred. The line of her firm jaw grew a little more obstinate and the light of prospective adventure flickered in her eyes. I saw that she was determined to go and to mingle with the crowd. She may have intellectual powers above the average, which scare the frivolous until they know her, but at heart she is very, very young. So that when two French girls asked her to make one of the party they were arranging to go to the Carnival she joyfully accepted, and off they all started at an early hour in the overcrowded motor bus to Nice.

155

I had made no more objections, but I gave her a warning that she would probably be caught and kissed by every Tom, Dick, and Harry. I had watched the crowd during a Carnival in Cannes and had noticed that the favourite game had been for a band of perhaps thirty or forty young men to join hands and make a circle around any attractive girl and not to let her escape until their prisoner had been kissed by them all.

I had once been put in charge of four pretty girls by their sedate grandmother, who made me promise not to let them loose from her huge Rolls-Royce, in which we were all driven down to the harbour to see the fireworks. But directly her back was turned I was subjected to the fire of four pairs of pleading eyes and a battery of arguments which I found hard to resist.

"Oh, Lady Peg! Couldn't we just get out and have a *little* walk round? It's *so* dull just sitting in the car. If you came with us *what* could possibly happen? We could take Davis (the *chauffeur*) to protect us if you like."

At that moment a large but obviously male figure disguised as a woman leaped into the seat beside the *chauffeur* and half strangled the shocked and protesting man with fervent embraces. At the same moment I saw the Circle Game begin, and I decided that I *must* be firm and obey Grannie. If I let those pretty things loose in such a mad crowd I knew they would be separated from me at once and not seen again till next morning — if then. I could see that they longed to be pursued, captured, and kissed; and now, the expression of the

Gazelle was in no way shocked, but rather excited as I told her this story.

Well, the Carnival procession in Nice was to be in the afternoon — also there is said to be safety in numbers, and my Gazelle would be one of a party of six girls. I hoped that she would be in no way scared or disillusioned.

I need have had no fears. She returned late in the evening having madly enjoyed every moment of her day. The six girls had bought six little paper caps made in imitation of those worn by French sailors. These they wore at jaunty angles and six abreast marched down the *Avenue de la Victoire* — of course the cynosure of all eyes. They were bombarded with flowers and confetti and kissed in turn by innumerable sailors from the French ships in port. They bought bags of confetti for themselves, and the Gazelle confessed to me that she had met a pompous old gentleman with a protruding shelf and a very bald head. No speck of confetti disfigured his immaculate appearance and she, being taller than he, could not resist showering a handful of it upon his shining pate as he passed her. She even sprinkled with confetti the heads of *gendarmes* controlling the traffic, and they had taken her impertinence in the true Carnival spirit, merely grinning and shaking their all-powerful baton at the little minx as she danced on her way. When the procession of grotesque figures surrounding the most gigantic of them all — King Carnival — passed by, the Gazelle could not resist stuffing confetti into the eye-holes and aperture for the mouth, which, the figure being so huge, were

157

placed in the stomach, thereby surely nearly stifling the unfortunate man inside.

All this was poured forth to me by my excited Gazelle, who admitted that she had forgotten all her English dignity for one glorious day and had fully entered into the Carnival spirit of France. Just as it should be, and I wish more English tourists would forget their reserve when they come to play in Provence.

I shall always remember one dreary New Year's Day because of the one funny little incident it afforded. It was during the life-time of *Monsieur.* The pound sterling had collapsed, and all the English were told that they must be patriotic and spend their holidays at home rather than squander sorely needed money in sunnier climates. Some friends of ours, longing for sunshine and flowers, decided to be unpatriotic and to spend January in Cannes. They were to drive across France, and begged us to meet them at the Carlton Hotel for luncheon on New Year's Day. It rarely snows in the South, but it had been snowing, and we shivered outside the hotel as we awaited our friends' arrival, which we knew would be fairly punctual, as the car was to be driven by their son, an air ace of the 1914-18 war and a marvellous *chauffeur.*

Only ten minutes behind time the car drew up before the Carlton. It was plastered with snow and the windscreen was frozen over. The intrepid driver had risked the route through the High Alps, and his poor Mamma looked half-dead with fright and cold. With the aid of his father he helped her out of the car, then dived into it to fetch a large cheap-looking paper bag — which burst as he handed it to John. The entrance to the hotel was peppered with pipes — briar pipes!

"Your birthday present in advance, John!" he called out jubilantly. "You asked for a briar pipe from Woolworths, so I brought you a supply — four dozen."

My Man was terribly cruel and careless with pipes. He knocked them out on stone walls, fireplaces, and the studded soles of boots; he lost them continually when gardening, and when in the early days of our marriage I presented him with a marvellous Dunhill pipe he stared at it with positive dislike and said reproachfully: "Oh, darling, I *wish* you hadn't given me that expensive thing. I shall have to take care of it."

After which I bought him flawed briar pipes from Woolworths for sixpence or a shilling each, realising that what he needed was quantity rather than quality. This preference of his for the pipes supplied by Woolworths became known, and our friend had indeed pampered it. With joy I watched the expression of sheer amazement on the face of the pompous Commissionaire of the Carlton as that *pluie des pipes* showered around him, and with difficulty I suppressed my mirth as he, bound by the rule of politeness to every visitor, stretched his over-tight gold-braided uniform nearly forty-eight times to collect John's scattered gift from the slushy pavement.

Our luncheon that day was a dismal affair. We tried to be merry, and the son gallantly seconded our efforts, but the springs of geniality in his parents were frozen stiff. We were the only people lunching in the large

159

dining-hall, gazing at a depressing row of naked uncooked turkeys waiting in vain to be ordered by clients that never came. No turkey was provided for us, and our spirits sank even lower when we were given the ordinary lunch of soup, veal, and cheese. Food and drink are not vital to me — except caviare and coffee — and I could still chuckle inwardly over those pipes so that I came off best.

Gifts for the New Year can, as you see, take curious forms in France. A friend of mine, a *chic* and pretty American, with all the American spirit and invincible will to succeed in whatever she tries to do, acquired a white Alpine goat possessing the same characteristics. It was at the time of acute milk shortage when what meagre supply of this precious fluid was available had to be reserved for the children. To keep one's own goat and be sure of one's own milk and, if a really good goat, of occasional jugs of cream, a small pat of butter or a diminutive cheese became the fashion. Personally I have steadily resisted goats ever since 1930, when *Monsieur* and I finally dug up our roots from English soil and came to live in Provence. Goats have to be milked night and morning — by whom, I asked myself, and decided that it would most probably be by *Madame*. A *bonne-à-tout-faire* has her hands overfull already without loading them further with the urgent udder of a goat. Also she has her days-off and her annual holiday. Or she may become so deeply attached to the goat that she spends her days with it and neglects her household work. I've seen that happen. Before she bought a house of her own, my American friend and her husband hired the *Château* of a noble (English) Marquis, who, loving light and colour, had the floors white-tiled throughout, risking, as he confided to me, the possible comment that it might look like the public lavatories in Piccadilly. She then invested in a *bonne* — and a goat. The *bonne* became passionately attached to that goat to the exclusion of all else. Her cuisine suffered and meals were sketchy. The larder of the Marquis also suffered, because it was used as a stable, so that Francine could comfort her Beloved on wet days and tuck her up cosily at night. I should NOT like a goat kept in my larder. Also goats are voracious things and eat anything and everything. My property is not enormous and my olive trees under which the scanty pasture grows are planted fairly close together. One tethers the goat by a long chain, and I should be obliged to have a very short one or the goat would ring the bark of my precious trees and devour the lower slender twigs which they adore. My goat, if I had one, would certainly break loose and devour my vegetables and flowers, and I take great pride in my garden and value my gardener. I should miss these assets more than I like to own, and I could not allow a goat to rob me of such treasures.

Lastly, during the great heat of July and August nearly all pasturage dries up unless constantly watered, and in this district water can be scarce. And I flatly refuse to exercise any goat on a chain or to allow it to crop the hedges of unsuspecting neighbours, as is sometimes done by desperate people.

And so I have remained goat-less, and when my pretty American friend, installed in her own house, boasted of her acquisition of a lovely white lady, sold to her cheaply because it had horns, I was not very enthusiastic.

Some days later I could not resist telephoning to ask her how she and her goat were faring — and what her English husband thought about it.

"Well — I know nothing at all about goats," she began, "and I must own that I rather dreaded my *bonne's* day out as I knew I'd have to milk mine in the evening. I made Charles swear he'd keep that day free so he could help me! Well, at least I knew at which end of the goat to begin. She didn't like me and kept trying to butt me with those frightening horns, but Charles was splendid and tickled her nose with an olive twig — oh! bless you for telling me goats adored them! — this kept her quieter, but for a long time she wouldn't give me a drop of milk. But I became as cussed as she was, and I pulled and I tugged as it seemed for hours till I *did* get *some,* but only enough for our *café-au-lait* for the morning. I got fearfully cramped crouching down, and in the end I lay on my back under her, protected from her back heels by the bucket, and went on hauling from that position. But I *did* milk her, as I swore I would if I had to stay there all day. Now I'm getting quite good as a milker, so good that my *bonne* suggests that it would be a good idea if *Madame* undertook the milking of the goat for always. But I'm wondering if it *is* a good idea. What do you think?"

"Most definitely a VERY BAD idea," I stated firmly. "You're too ornamental an element of our small Anglo-American Colony to cloister yourself with a goat, and it would amount to that. Remember those daily morning and evening sessions! Think of the tie! You'd have to give up all cocktail parties [she adores them] and your winter sports in Switzerland, and —"

"Yes, I see you're right," she broke in. "Even if I have to get in extra help (and she had to), my *bonne* had better be responsible for the goat."

That was a long time ago. The goats were multiplied and the young couple boasted of their CREAM. Charles loves good food, and his wife is a very clever cook, and thenceforth supplemented the efforts of her *bonne* to produce luscious *entremets* for the delectation of her husband and guests, who all uncomfortably wondered whether they should launch forth on goats, doubting that they had the courage of their enterprising American hostess. But then the summer came, the *grande chaleur* began — and so did bathing picnics and summer galas. The days-off of the *bonne* could never be forgotten. Finally there came her fortnight's holiday . . .

I wasn't in the least surprised when I returned from a holiday in England to hear that the goats had been disposed of. It seemed to be a sore subject, so I never asked why, when, or where.

But to return to the New Year in Provence. We English living in the mountains prefer to do our entertaining in our own homes rather than frequent the luxurious hotels on the coast. Galas are all very well in their way and I have enjoyed several in the past, but they are ruinously expensive and all much alike. The dinner tickets, costing some thousands of francs, do not include wine — on these occasions the biggest item of all. Then lovely girls drift up to your table and cajole you to buy tombola tickets for prizes of model gowns, jewellery, perhaps even a motor car presented by important Paris houses. The dancing-floor is too full for any enjoyment; the crowd generally so great that often one is unable to identify one's friends or even to see and appreciate the lovely dresses of the women in so seething a mob.

At home one can keep up a sustained conversation with a special friend, admire her frock, note the recipe of some delicious dish she has most probably prepared with her own hands.

To such a New Year's party did I go last year, given by the old friend I call "The Lady of the Kennels" in my last book.[1] She has achieved the miniature castle of her dreams, and in her large and lovely living-room, with its pale magnolia-tinted walls, its floor of rose-pink bricks forming a parquet pattern, its arched brick fireplace in which a fire of olive-logs blazed, she joyously received about thirty English and Americans for preliminary cocktails and a marvellous buffet-supper she had cooked and presented with her own hands; for war-experience in England taught her to cook and her enjoyment of good food to learn how to make every dish perfect.

As I walked down her long stairway, which is built in this great room so that its hand-wrought banisters of old iron, scrolled and twisted into a lovely design, form its greatest ornament, I could look down upon many old friends already assembled there, and admire the effect of

---

[1] "Beauty for Ashes" (Messrs William Blackwood & Sons Ltd., 1948).

shaded lights falling upon bowls of scarlet carnations. Light gleamed through red Bohemian glass, and the great fire of olive-logs glowed and flamed in the open fireplace.

There was a cheerful noise already, yes, definitely a noise, always the sign of a successful party, our hostess is so full of *joie-de-vivre* that she infects others, and it was lovely and heart-warming to be spied and welcomed, then drawn down into the midst of so many people that I have learned to love. By special request of my hostess I was wearing a scarlet dress sprigged with little white flowers, copied from an ancient Provençal dress, with a little tight high-waisted bodice, a foamy *fichu*, sleeves tight from the wrist to elbow and developing into balloons at the shoulder; the tremendously full skirt shirred over the hips and falling to the scarlet-sandalled feet, worn over a voluminous white petticoat, ancient and handworked, starched beyond belief to hold out the flowered skirt above it — an heirloom lent to me for that occasion to make the dress perfect. In our circle, if we admire each other's clothes we say so, and everyone was very kind about my dress. At least it harmonised with my hostess's colour-scheme. The crowd thickened, the drinks were passed round, and the usual non-alcoholic fruit juice specially procured for me; the noise increased, everyone was wishing everyone else a happy New Year — it was beginning happily anyway — and I was surrounded by men, laughing and chaffing each other and me, when my hostess standing nearby said suddenly, "Génie (my French nickname), LOOK DOWN!" I looked down and found my feet had disappeared beneath a white foam of — PETTICOAT! It had come unmoored and surrounded me on the floor.

A man had whispered to my hostess, looking sidelong at me, "Is that — normal?" and then she warned me of my predicament.

I couldn't pull it up and fix it in public, and so — I just skipped out of it, and with assumed *sang-froid* proceeded to point out the rare beauties of its workmanship to my laughing audience.

So do we skip out of all foolish formalities in our lovely land of Provence.

CHAPTER
TEN

Laughter, The Divine Disinfectant

Again, I quote the immortal Elizabeth of the German Garden. In one of her books she spoke of laughter as "that divine disinfectant, that heavenly purge," and all through my life I have proved over and over again the truth of that profound remark.

How often has a flood of laughter washed away bitterness, turned away wrath, saved a difficult situation, enabled one to regain one's lost sense of proportion and the true values in life, and, above all, given one a perception of one's own foolishness! If one can only see the ridiculous side of ONESELF and one's behaviour all danger is past.

Lately more and more of the English have escaped to Provence and, once here, often want to stay for ever. They get so much for nothing (I refer to the things of the spirit, for material things could hardly be more costly than they are now): sunshine, flowers, and fruits in lavish abundance; the majesty of mountains; the everlasting peace of olive groves, and the magic of the Mediterranean. For the sea is turquoise blue and pale

Nile green where it covers yellow sand, shading to a clear aquamarine merging into cobalt as it grows deeper, and a true amethyst where rocks are hid. Chiefly, I am sure, they want to stay because this is a land of laughter.

Every day there is some funny little saying or occurrence to amuse one, for the Provençal peasant is at heart just a great child, and where children are there is always light and laughter. Their original points of view, their *joie-de-vivre*, their complete naturalness and ignorance of the conventions, their spontaneity, the warm affection they give to those worthy of it — and their judgment is unerring — are found also in the Provençaux.

Here in Provence we get loving service. Our staffs (perhaps staves?) and our peasant friends who come in to help may not be conventional servants or, in the English sense, well trained, but they are hard working, ready to do any kind of work or to render any service to a visiting guest. They are undeterred by domestic catastrophes, and indeed rather enjoy them, and they respond so warmly to kindness, understanding or consideration.

Above all, oh! transcendentally above all, they have warm hearts and a lovely sense of humour; they can laugh and *do* laugh all day long, and they make you laugh too, and so life goes merrily on.

"Laughter, that divine disinfectant . . ."